LIBERATION OF PARIS 1944

Patton's race for the Seine

CAMPAIGN • 194

LIBERATION OF PARIS 1944

Patton's race for the Seine

STEVEN J ZALOGA ILLUSTRATED BY HOWARD GERRARD

Series editors Marcus Cowper and Nikolai Bogdanovic

First published in Great Britain in 2008 by Osprey Publishing,
Midland House, West Way, Botley, Oxford OX2 0PH, UK
443 Park Avenue South, New York, NY 10016, USA
E-mail: info@ospreypublishing.com

A CIP catalog record for this book is available from the British Library

ISBN: 978 1 84603 246 2

Editorial by Ilios Publishing Ltd, Oxford, UK (www.iliospublishing.com)
Page layout by The Black Spot
Index by Auriol Griffith-Jones
Typeset in Sabon and Myriad Pro
Maps by The Map Studio Ltd
3D bird's-eye views by The Black Spot
Originated by PPS Grasmere Ltd., Leeds
Printed in China through Worldprint

08 09 10 11 12   10 9 8 7 6 5 4 3 2 1

FOR A CATALOG OF ALL BOOKS PUBLISHED BY OSPREY MILITARY
AND AVIATION PLEASE CONTACT:

NORTH AMERICA
Osprey Direct, c/o Random House Distribution Center, 400 Hahn Road,
Westminster, MD 21157
E-mail: info@ospreydirect.com

ALL OTHER REGIONS
Osprey Direct UK, P.O. Box 140 Wellingborough, Northants, NN8 2FA, UK
E-mail: info@ospreydirect.co.uk

www.ospreypublishing.com

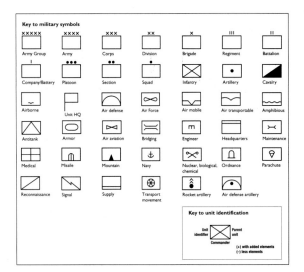

AUTHOR'S NOTE

The author would like to thank Paul Cardin, Xavier Lena and Yvan Garnier
for helping to track down the precise locations of several of the historical
photos used in this book.

GLOSSARY

AOK 1	Armee Oberkommando 1, the headquarters of the German First Army
COMAC	Comité d'Action Militaire, Military Action Committee, the military command of the CNR
CNR	Conseil National de la Résistance, Committee of National Resistance, the governing body of the French resistance
FFI	Forces Françaises de l'Intérieur, French Forces of the Interior, the French resistance army in France
FK	*Feldkommandantur*, field commands of the German occupation forces usually made up of military police and security units
FTP	Francs-Tireurs et Partisans: the French Communist armed resistance group
GT	*Groupements tactiques*, the French equivalent of US Army combat commands in armored divisions
GTD	The *groupement tactique* of the 2e DB under Colonel Dio
GTL	The *groupement tactique* of the 2e DB under Colonel Langlade
GTV	The *groupement tactique* of the 2e DB under Colonel Bilotte
OB West	Oberbefehlshaber West, the German Army's Western Front high command
OSS	Office of Special Services, the US equivalent of the British SOE and precursor of the CIA.
PCF	Parti Communiste Français, French Communist Party
RBFM	Régiment Blindé de Fusiliers Marins, Armored Regiment of Naval Riflemen, the tank destroyer battalion of the 2e DB
RMT	Régiment de Marche de Tchad, Chad March Regiment; the mechanized infantry of the 2e DB with three battalions
SOE	Special Operations Executive, the British organization responsible for supporting foreign resistance movements in continental Europe
2e DB	2e Division Blindée, French 2nd Armored Division
12e Cuir	12e Régiment de Cuirassiers, one of the 2e DB's three tank battalions
12e RCA	12e Régiment de Chasseurs d'Afrique, one of the 2e DB's three tank battalions
501e RCC	501e Régiment de Chars de Combat, 501st Tank Regiment, one of the 2e DB's three tank battalions

ARTIST'S NOTE

Readers may care to note that the original paintings from which the
battlescene color plates in this book were prepared are available for private
sale. All reproduction copyright whatsoever is retained by the Publishers.
All enquiries should be addressed to:

Howard Gerrard
11 Oaks Road
Tenterden
Kent
TN30 6RD
UK

The Publishers regret that they can enter into no correspondence
upon this matter.

CONTENTS

RENAULT · CAUDRON

EIFF

INTRODUCTION

"History has shown that the loss of Paris always means the fall of the whole of France." Adolf Hitler's remark provides a trenchant forecast of the fate of the Wehrmacht in France in the last two weeks of August 1944. Paris itself was neither a major Allied objective nor a major German strongpoint. The US Army planned to skirt around the city, isolating it without the need for a frontal assault to await its eventual surrender. The Wehrmacht, frantic for troops after its heavy summer losses, defended the city with a skeleton force. Instead, the liberation of Paris was initiated by the citizens of Paris; not an entirely spontaneous effort, but one that had little formal military preparation. The uprising in Paris in August 1944 might have ended in tragedy as befell Warsaw that same month. The fate of Paris rested heavily on the decisions of the German commander of Paris, General der Infanterie Dietrich von Choltitz, who had been ordered by Hitler to raze the city to the ground. Prompt Allied action and Choltitz' unwillingness to destroy one of Europe's great cities avoided a major battle for Paris. Rather than causing the end of the German occupation in France, the liberation of Paris was a symbolic conclusion to the collapse of the Wehrmacht in France in the last two weeks of August 1944.

THE STRATEGIC SITUATION

By the middle of August 1944, the situation of the Wehrmacht in France was dire. Although the German Army had managed to hold back the British attacks around Caen and the US attacks toward St. Lô in lower Normandy for nearly two months, the attrition of the June and July fighting took a severe toll on the German Seventh Army. On July 20, 1944, German officers attempted to kill Hitler at his headquarters in East Prussia. Although the bomb plot failed, it left Hitler physically weakened for several weeks, and deeply suspicious of the loyalty of the senior army leadership. Under these circumstances, he seized control over most key battlefield decisions, which only hastened the impending doom of the German Seventh Army.

When the US Army launched Operation *Cobra* on July 24, 1944, the brittle German defenses were shattered. The US Army had secretly added a second contingent to its forces in France, Patton's Third Army, which was specifically intended to accelerate the breakthrough. Patton's objective was to advance rapidly westward into Brittany to seize additional ports such as Brest. In one of the fastest armored advances of the war, US tank columns charged toward the Breton ports at Quiberon Bay and Brest against minimal German

RIGHT
In a scene typical of the fighting in the last two weeks of August, an M4A1 (76mm) tank races past a derelict German motorized column. The weakness of the Wehrmacht in the Paris–Orléans gap and the mobility of the US Army overwhelmed the defenses in front of Paris. (NARA)

BELOW RIGHT
US troops of the 80th Infantry Division enter Argentan on August 20, 1944. Bradley's decision to halt the US advance into the Falaise corridor at Argentan has remained the source of controversy. (NARA)

resistance. Hitler saw Patton's extended lines as a sign of weakness and as a potential opportunity for a reversal of German fortunes in Normandy. He ordered the Seventh Army to muster its dwindling Panzer force and direct it in a violent counterattack, Operation *Lüttich*, to cut off Patton's forces by pushing to the sea near Avranches. The plan was hopeless from the outset as the Panzer forces did not have the mobility to concentrate in the Avranches sector rapidly enough and, as a result, were obliged to conduct the attack starting on August 7 in a premature and disjointed fashion. US infantry stopped the attack almost immediately around Mortain. While German losses were not especially high, the diversion of the Panzer forces from the Caen sector enabled Montgomery's 21st Army Group to begin to roll up German defenses and to threaten a major envelopment of the Seventh Army around

The Operation *Dragoon* landings on the Mediterranean coast of southern France on August 15 delivered the *coup de grâce* to Wehrmacht plans to hold central France. Within days, Hitler had authorized a wholesale retreat from most of southern and central France. Here, troops of the 45th Infantry Division come ashore from LCIs. (NARA)

Falaise. Hitler had committed his mobile reserve in the wrong place at the wrong time, and the German Seventh Army would soon pay the price.

Although Operation *Lüttich* never seriously threatened the US advance into Brittany, Patton became convinced that this mission was fundamentally mistaken. The experience at Cherbourg in June 1944 made it clear that the Germans would demolish the ports before their capture, undermining their value as alternative supply points. Brest intact was priceless; Brest in shambles had little immediate value; the prospects for capturing Brest intact were slim in spite of the lightning speed of the advance. Instead, Patton urged Bradley to change the plan and permit him to re-orient the bulk of his forces back eastward toward Germany. Patton saw the ultimate objective of the summer fighting to be a fast advance over the Seine River, and by mid-August, no appreciable German forces stood in his path. With the Panzer threat contained at Mortain, Eisenhower began to appreciate the opportunities for a rapid dash toward the Seine that would complete a deep envelopment of the German Seventh Army and precipitate its rout. On August 8, Patton was authorized to re-orient his forces eastward, leaving only a corps in Brittany.

By the second week of August, the German Seventh Army was on the verge of becoming encircled by the British/Canadian thrust emanating from Caen, and the rapidly advancing US mechanized columns farther south around Argentan. Rather than permit an organized retreat to re-establish a coherent new defense line on the Seine, Hitler ordered another Panzer counterattack to blunt the Allied advance. While the fate of the Seventh Army played itself out in the fields south of Falaise, the fate of the three other German armies in France were about to be thrown into the balance. The First Army on the Atlantic coast, the Fifteenth Army on the Pas de Calais, and the Nineteenth Army in southern France had been weakened by the need to send reinforcements to the embattled Seventh Army in Normandy. On August 10, the German First Army was asked to do the impossible, to create a new

"Is Paris burning?" demanded Hitler of his generals on August 24, 1944. Although there were many fires in the city during the fighting, it did not reach the apocalyptic proportions ordered by Hitler. This view was taken by a US Army photographer from eastern Paris with St. Clotilde church to the right, smoke from the Grand Palais fire in the center and the dome of St. Augustin to the left. (NARA)

defensive line between Alençon and the Loire Valley to halt Patton's advance. With its forces stretched thin along the Atlantic coast, it depended on the other armies to send it the necessary divisions. Given the state of the French railways and Allied air supremacy, this was impossible.

The German predicament in France went from dire to catastrophic on August 15, 1944, when a second Allied invasion, Operation *Dragoon*, took place on the Riviera. The amphibious landings by the US Seventh Army on France's Mediterranean coast were not seriously opposed by the understrength German Nineteenth Army, and US columns began making a rapid advance northward. Clearly, the strategic aim was to meet up with Allied forces in central France, essentially trapping the German First and Nineteenth Armies. By the second week of August, not only was the Seventh Army in Normandy on the brink of destruction, but the entire German occupation of France was threatened.

OPPOSING COMMANDERS

The demoralization of the Wehrmacht was no more evident than in the fate of Generalfeldmarschall Günther Hans von Kluge, in command of the German Army in the West. Despondent over the destruction of the Seventh Army in the Falaise Gap, and suspected of involvement in the bomb plot against Hitler, he committed suicide on August 18. (MHI)

WEHRMACHT

Adolf Hitler played a critical role in the tactical decisions affecting the campaign in France. His injury in the July 20 bomb plot temporarily limited his involvement in day-to-day command in late July, but by early August, he was again taking an active role in tactical command. The bomb plot left him deeply suspicious of the regular army, and increasingly reliant on the Nazi stalwarts of the Waffen-SS. It also amplified his predilection for nihilistic tantrums, and his tactical style soon became dominated by "stand fast or die" orders. So in the case of the fortified ports along the Atlantic Wall, Hitler ordered their garrisons to remain in place even after it became evident that they would be cut off by Allied forces. As a result, about a quarter-million troops were left behind when the Wehrmacht finally retreated from France in late August. Hitler was also disinclined to permit the construction of secondary defensive lines, for fear that they would only encourage the army to retreat sooner. The psychological effects of this tactical style on the Wehrmacht are debatable, but the most important consequence was that once the front began to collapse, retreat quickly degenerated into rout. The bomb plot had extensive repercussions in the high command of the Wehrmacht in France owing to the important role played by several key figures.

The German armed forces in the west were under the direction of the OB West (Oberbefehlshaber West), commanded by Generalfeldmarschall Gerd von Rundstedt until July 2, 1944, when Hitler relieved him for proposing to withdraw German forces to more defensible positions in Normandy out of the range of naval gunfire. He was replaced by Günther Hans von Kluge, a favorite of Hitler for his leadership of the Fourth Army during the envelopment of the French forces through the Ardennes in 1940. Kluge had a distinguished record on the Eastern Front but was seriously injured in an automobile accident in October 1943. He was nicknamed "Clever Hans" for his political opportunism and vacillation. He was aware of earlier plots against Hitler, and was privy to the July 20 plot. The plotters contacted him shortly after the attack on Hitler, but he refused to throw in his lot with them until Hitler's fate was certain. His last-minute vacillation led to the collapse of the plot in France and the execution of most of the key plotters. He remained fearful that the German police would discover his involvement, and Gestapo interrogations of one of his former aides increased his concern. Expecting to be arrested, Kluge committed suicide on 18 August. Hitler's miracle worker, the ruthless Walter Model, replaced him.

During the Normandy campaign, OB West commanded two major formations, Army Group B under Generalfeldmarschall Erwin Rommel and Army Group G under Generaloberst Johannes Blaskowitz. Army Group B included the Seventh Army in Normandy and the Fifteenth Army on the Pas de Calais while Army Group G included the First Army on the Atlantic coast and Nineteenth Army on the Mediterranean. Rommel was seriously wounded on July 17, 1944, when a Spitfire strafed his staff car and Kluge took over direct command of Army Group B shortly after. The Seventh Army had been commanded by Generaloberst Friedrich Dollmann, who died of a heart attack on June 29, 1944. To direct the campaign in Normandy better, the Seventh Army was split in two. The reconstituted Seventh Army corresponded to the American sector of the front, and Panzergruppe West was stationed opposite the British and Canadian sector.

Besides the tactical command structure in France, there was a separate military government for occupied France (Militärbefelshaber in Frankreich) under General der Infanterie Karl-Heinrich von Stülpnagel, which controlled four military administrative districts as well as a separate Greater Paris command (Militärverwaltungs-Bezirk Gross Paris), commanded by Generalleutnant Hans von Boineberg-Lengsfeld. The areas of northwest France near Paris came under the command of the Militärverwaltungs-Bezirk Nordwest Frankreich under Generalleutnant Erwin Vierow, consisting of 15 field commands (Feldkommandantur) based in the major cities. Besides the military occupation forces in France, there were two other separate security organizations, the Sipo-SD police force (Sicherheitspolizei-Sicherheitsdienst) and the Higher SS and Police Command—France (HSSPF: Höhere SS und Polizeiführer Frankreich). Relations between the leaders of the military occupation forces and the German police were strained as the army commanders found that the brutal police tactics stirred popular unrest and complicated their occupation duties. The Milice, a Vichy French militia force, supported the German police most ardently. The regular French police carried out most ordinary police work but were not widely trusted by the Germans as they were infiltrated by resistance sympathizers.

The military governor of France, Gen. von Stülpnagel was intimately involved in the bomb plot, and on July 20 ordered the arrests of the senior SS and SD chiefs in Paris. The police arrests were short lived, as Kluge relieved Stülpnagel as soon as it was clear that Hitler had survived the bomb blast. He was replaced by General der Luftwaffe Karl Kitzinger on July 31, 1944, who played little role in the subsequent Paris fighting. Many other key officers in the German occupation force were also involved in the bomb plot, including the Paris commander Gen.Lt. von Boineberg.

Boineberg was replaced by General der Infanterie Dietrich von Choltitz who would prove to be the most critical German commander in the eventual fate of Paris. Prior to his appointment to Paris, Choltitz had been in command of 84.Korps in Normandy facing the US Army. Choltitz had begun the war as an infantry battalion commander in the Polish campaign, receiving the Iron Cross and he was decorated again with the Knights Cross for his performance in the 1940 France campaign. He became commander of the 16.Infanterie Regiment after France, and was decorated again with the German Cross in Gold in February 1942 for his leadership in the Russian campaign. After his regiment's performance in the siege of Sevastopol in the summer of 1942, he rose to divisional command in August 1942 and to corps command in December 1942. In early 1944, he was transferred to Italy to lead 76.Panzer Korps during the attempts to crush the Anzio beachhead. He was assigned command of 84.Korps on June 15, 1944, which was stationed in the western sector of the Normandy front, resisting the American advance around St. Lô. On August 7, 1944, he was ordered to report directly to Hitler, and was given the assignment as commander of "Festung Paris." Hitler made it quite clear that position was no longer an occupation mission but rather the defense of city. As a result, Choltitz not only commanded Wehrmacht forces in Paris, but separate organizations such as the police, and other German government organizations were placed directly under his command. Although Choltitz was honored by his new appointment, he was deeply shaken by his meeting with Hitler. The Führer was obviously suffering from the medical effects of the bomb blast, and at times seemed to be mentally deranged. Instead of imbuing Choltitz with new enthusiasm, the meeting with Hitler left him disillusioned and despondent, eventually having important consequences in his choices for the fate of Paris. Gen.Lt. von Boineberg's assessment of Choltitz on meeting him in Paris for the first time was that he was a "tough guy."

On August 10, a day after Choltitz arrived in Paris, yet another command change took place affecting the city. With the Seventh Army largely trapped in Normandy, the First Army on the Atlantic coast gradually had its assignment extended to cover the exposed southern flank through the Loire Valley. In late July after the US Operation *Cobra* breakthrough, it was assigned to set up blocking positions on the Loire River between Orléans and Nantes. When Patton's forces began their race toward the Seine, First Army's assignment was extended on August 10 to create a defensive perimeter from Alençon and the Loire River valley to the perimeter of the Seventh Army with the aim of blocking an American advance toward the upper Seine. The First Army headquarters, AOK 1 (Armee Oberkommando 1) had an impossible task attempting to control operations in the Loire Valley from its coastal headquarters in Bordeaux, so, as an expedient, the headquarters' Ia (Operations Section) under Oberstleutnant Emmerich was sent to form a regional headquarters at Fontainebleau, later dubbed "General z.b.V. AOK 1"

General der Infanterie Dietrich von Choltitz, hero of Sevastopol and former commander of 84.Korps in Normandy, was Hitler's pick to command Festung Paris in August 1944. (NARA)

Charles de Gaulle is seen here at the Arc de Triomphe on August 25 with two of the senior resistance leaders, Georges Bidault on the left who headed the CNR, and Alexandre Parodi on the extreme right, who was de Gaulle's personal representative on the resistance committee. (NARA)

(z.b.V.= *zur besonderen Verwendung*: for special purpose). Although nominally in command of the tactical formations in advance of Paris as well as the Paris garrison, it was so poorly equipped with signals equipment that Choltitz instead went directly to Army Group B headquarters for instructions.

Choltitz did not actually receive command of Paris until August 14, when Gen.Lt. von Boineberg was belatedly relieved of command after his role in the bomb plot became suspected. One of Choltitz' first actions was to try to impose unity of command over the Paris defenses. There was some overlap of authority as Gen.Lt. Vierow's headquarters controlled some of the field commands of police and security units in the districts around Paris. With Kluge's approval, Vierow was dismissed as Military Commander, Northwest France, and he reverted to his secondary role as commander of the improvised Armee Korps Somme. Vierow's chief of staff Generalmajor Hubertus von Aulock, was assigned to lead the defenses on the western and southern approaches of Paris based on the local field commands. Choltitz was also given authority over all German military and civilian administrations in the city, although in practice this proved to be almost impossible to carry out as, under the chaotic conditions in the city in mid-August, most of the administrative headquarters in the city were intent on escaping regardless of Choltitz's instructions.

FREE FRENCH FORCES

Since 1940, Charles de Gaulle had attempted to organize an alternative to Pétain's discredited Vichy government. De Gaulle despised the partisan politics of interwar France and attempted to create an apolitical movement motivated by French patriotism. This was hardly unusual in European politics of the time, paralleling other national saviors like Pilsudski in Poland, Mannerheim in Finland, Horthy in Hungary and Ataturk in Turkey, or for that matter, Pétain's assumption of power in 1940 to redeem the defeat of the French Army. De Gaulle eventually created a coalition of political parties linked to his army in exile. To acquire some measure of political legitimacy, de Gaulle needed the support of the French resistance, which through 1942 was scattered and weak. De Gaulle preferred a centrally controlled resistance movement led by military officers, but most armed resistance groups emerged from political parties and trade unions, especially those of the left. De Gaulle was especially suspicious of the communist PCF (Parti Communiste Français), but recognized their central role in the resistance. He was careful to cultivate their support, reinforcing this with friendly relations with Stalin and the Soviet Union. Communist support was crucial in de Gaulle's efforts to unify the major resistance groups under the CNR (Conseil National de la Résistance) in May 1943, headed first by Jean Moulin and, after his betrayal, by Georges Bidault. Although the CNR was the nominal political leadership of the unified FFI (Forces Françaises de l'Intérieur), in reality the resistance groups retained their autonomy. Leadership of the resistance in Paris was a collaborative affair, with the CNR attempting to arrive at a consensus. The COMAC (Comité d'Action Militaire) was the CNR's military command. In 1944, de Gaulle created the État Major FFI under the command of Général Marie Pierre Koenig to integrate the FFI into the Allied military command structure, but this organization was initially focused on coordinating the numerous armed partisan groups in rural France that had been supported by the British SOE (Special Operations Executive).

In June 1944, COMAC appointed "Colonel Rol" as commander of the FFI P1 region, that is the Île de France region including Paris and the departments of Seine, Seine-et-Oise and Seine-et-Marne. Rol was the wartime pseudonym of Georges René Henri Tanguy, a 38-year-old sheet-metal worker who had worked at various Paris area automotive plants before the war, frequently dismissed for his Communist Party agitation. He went to Spain in 1937, serving as the political commissar of the 14th International Brigade, and served in the French Army in 1940. Rol-Tanguy's selection as the head of the FFI forces around Paris was a tacit recognition that the Communist Party had the largest and best-organized armed groups in and around the city. Even so, they numbered barely 600 armed insurgents.

The French army commander most closely associated with the Paris operation was Philippe François Marie, vicomte de Hauteclocque, better known by his wartime pseudonym of Jacques Leclerc. He came from an aristocratic family with a long tradition of military service going back to the Fifth Crusade. Leclerc entered the army through St. Cyr and Saumur as a young cavalry officer in 1925, eventually being posted to various units in the North African colonies and seeing combat in local pacification campaigns. Although appointed to a prestigious teaching post at St. Cyr, he itched to take part in a major campaign and during summer vacation in 1933 set off for Morocco. Although recommended for the Légion d'Honneur for his leadership of an irregular partisan formation during the fighting, the award was delayed by senior officers who did not appreciate his excessive zeal. During the 1940 campaign, he served as a captain on the headquarters staff of the 4e Division d'Infanterie, and escaped rather than surrendering. After hearing one of de Gaulle's radio broadcasts calling for French patriots to rally to his cause in England, Leclerc managed to reach London via Spain. He was an odd man out among de Gaulle's officers who were mostly reservists; most professional officers with aristocratic backgrounds had remained in France and supported Pétain's collaborationist Vichy government. De Gaulle was attempting to bring the French colonies in Equatorial Africa under his movement, and Leclerc's first assignment was to stage a coup in Cameroon. Deserted by the Senegalese troops assigned his mission, Leclerc and two-dozen French soldiers managed to reach the capital of Douala by canoe with British assistance. Leclerc proclaimed himself military governor in the name of de Gaulle's Free French government, and the coup succeeded after the commander of the city's garrison, Capitaine Louis Dio, sided with him. Leclerc's next assignment was to seize control of neighboring Gabon, which had opted to side with Pétain's government. The campaign lasted a month

The primary French commander for the Paris operation was Général Jacques Leclerc, commander of the French 2e Division Blindée, seen here to the left on August 23 after his advance guard had reached Rambouillet. (NARA)

and was the culmination of de Gaulle's seizure of the French Equatorial African colonies. In view of his remarkable successes, de Gaulle assigned Leclerc his most difficult assignment, the seizure of Chad, held by an Italian garrison centered at the fortress town of Kufra. Leclerc's force consisted of 100 French and 200 African troops, and about 100 vehicles. On January 31, 1941, the column set off on a journey of nearly 1,000 miles across the Sahara with the main body arriving outside Kufra on February 17. After fighting off an Italian motorized company with air support, Leclerc laid siege to the fort, which surrendered on March 1. For the next year, Leclerc's forces staged raids against Italian garrisons farther north, culminating in another epic march across the Sahara in December 1942 to overwhelm the Italian garrisons in the Fezzan region of southwest Libya in support of Montgomery's El Alamein offensive. After overwhelming several Italian garrisons, Leclerc's force met the British Eighth Army in mid-February. Renamed "L Force," the French detachment fought in Tunisia, distinguishing itself to the extent that Montgomery honored it as the lead formation in the victory parade in Tunis. At the end of the North Africa campaign, L Force served as the seed of the new 2e Division Française Libre, what would become the legendary 2e Division Blindée. In view of Leclerc's loyalty and obvious military talents, he was promoted to *général* and assigned to train the new division in Rabat, Morocco. Leclerc's relations with the senior French commanders of the First French Army training in North Africa was strained. Leclerc made no secret of the fact that he viewed them as opportunists who had collaborated with the Germans and switched to the Allies only after the US Army seized French North Africa in November 1942; they viewed him as a troublesome little upstart captain. De Gaulle had been lobbying Eisenhower to assign at least one French division to any operations in northwest France in the hope that such a unit would lead any Allied advance into Paris. Leclerc's division was the obvious choice, and it was transported to England in April 1944.

US ARMY

The US Army's 12th Army Group was commanded by General Omar Bradley, a classmate of Eisenhower's from the US Military Academy at West Point class of 1915. Both were from mid-Western farm families with no military tradition and were younger than most of their subordinate commanders, such as George Patton and Leonard Gerow. Neither had served in combat with the American Expeditionary Force in World War I, but had risen to senior command as staff officers because of their managerial and planning skills. Bradley had raised the new 82nd Division in 1942, and Eisenhower had sent him to North Africa in February 1943 after the debacle at Kasserine Pass, serving as deputy commander of II Corps under General George S. Patton. During the campaign on Sicily, Bradley served as a corps commander, part of Patton's Seventh Army. Patton's impetuous behavior landed him in political trouble after Sicily, and so it was Bradley rather than the older Patton who received command of the US First Army for the invasion of Normandy. Following Operation *Cobra* on July 24, 1944, the US contingent in France expanded to include Patton's Third Army, and Bradley was selected by Eisenhower to take over as the new 12th Army Group commander.

Major-General Leonard Gerow commanded V Corps at Omaha Beach and was the senior Allied commander for the liberation of Paris. (NARA)

Eisenhower's and Bradley's managerial style of command and the relative lack of political interference from Washington led to relative indifference about Paris in US planning. This is in stark contrast to the Italian theater where Winston Churchill's political interests and General Mark Clark's vainglorious ambitions placed central importance on the capture of Rome in June 1944. Both Bradley and Eisenhower regarded the capture of Paris as a logistical nuisance and distraction, rather than as a splendid opportunity for martial glory.

The last-minute decision to race for Paris was assigned to Major-General Leonard Gerow's V Corps. Gerow was a few years older than Bradley, graduating from the Virginia Military Institute in 1911. He served in the Mexican campaign in 1916, and as a signals officer in France in 1918 where he was involved in the early use of the radio by the US Army. He graduated first of his class from the Advanced Course at Fort Benning's Infantry School; second was Bradley. He subsequently attended the US Army Command and General Staff School where Eisenhower was his study partner; Eisenhower graduated first, Gerow 11th. He later commanded Eisenhower in 1941 while heading the war plans division of the general staff. Following the outbreak of the war, he commanded the newly formed 29th Division that would later serve under his corps command at Omaha Beach. The V Corps was the first large US Army formation created in Britain for the Allied invasion of France, and Eisenhower picked Gerow for its command in July 1943. As a result, he was deeply involved in planning for the D-Day invasion, and V Corps was assigned Omaha Beach. He was highly regarded by both Eisenhower and Bradley though not especially popular with his subordinate divisional commanders owing to his propensity for micromanaging operations. He had a very difficult time dealing with Leclerc, failing to appreciate the dual loyalties burdening the French commander—to both de Gaulle and his nominal superiors in the US Army. This would lead to a very unhappy command relationship for both generals during the Paris operation.

The right man in the right place. Lieutenant-General George S. Patton displayed his cavalryman's aptitude for speed and daring during the Third Army's incredible race for the Seine. It is doubtful that more conservative generals like Hodges of First Army would have conducted the campaign in such a freewheeling and successful fashion. (NARA)

OPPOSING PLANS

GERMAN PLANS

German planning in the last two weeks of August 1944 was primarily concerned with attempting to stave off disaster. Not only was the Seventh Army and Panzergruppe West on the verge of envelopment in the Falaise pocket, but both First Army and Nineteenth Army were about to be cut off by the US invasion of southern France. Paris was an afterthought in most German strategic planning as Berlin had poor intelligence on US operations in the Loire Valley and continually underestimated the mobility of the US Army in the hands of skilled cavalrymen like Patton.

Plans for the defense of Paris can be divided into two distinct sectors, the outer defenses of Gen. z.b.V. AOK 1 and the inner defenses of Festung Paris. Plans for the outer sector were improvised because of the lack of resources. The intention on August 15, 1944, was to create a blocking position from Orléans to Gien, folding back toward the Seine River at Montargis and Nemours to hold the Seine River southeast of Paris. In addition, an outer blocking position was planned for the Chartres area to cover the

In mid-August 1944, catastrophe awaited the Wehrmacht in France with most of Seventh Army encircled near Falaise. This field near Argentan is littered with the helmets and equipment abandoned by a German unit prior to their capture on August 20. (NARA)

southwestern approaches to Paris. To accomplish this, AOK 1 was promised the 49.Infanterie Division from Fifteenth Army on the Pas de Calais, and the 338.Infanterie Division from the Nineteenth Army on the Mediterranean; there was also some discussion of transferring the 18.Luftwaffe Felddivision from the Pas de Calais. The US Army spearheads arrived in this sector around August 18 before a comprehensive defense could be formed.

German plans for the defense of Festung Paris were constrained by the lack of troops to defend the city. Although the Paris garrison included well over 100,000 personnel at its peak, the vast majority of these were administrative personnel assigned to the numerous headquarters in the city. When Hitler appointed Choltitz as Paris commander on August 7 he ordered him to evacuate any "useless" administrative personnel, and to convert the able-bodied men into combatants. In reality, evacuation had been going on for days before Choltitz arrived in Paris with little central control.

To discourage any response to the evacuation from the Parisians, Hitler had also ordered the head of the SS in France, SS-Brigadeführer Karl Oberg, to enact a policy of collective reprisal for any French partisan activity under which a number of civilians would be killed for any acts of sabotage or combat action against German troops. In conjunction with their lackeys in the French Milice, the Gestapo and other German police organizations stepped up their efforts against the French resistance in mid-August, with a noticeable increase in summary executions.

Prior to the D-Day landings, the army's defense of Paris was primarily focused on maintenance of order and prevention of sabotage. Hitler discouraged the creation of any tactical defenses behind the main lines through the middle of the summer of 1944 for fear that it would only encourage retreat. Lacking any directives from Berlin, Gen.Lt. von Boineberg began to plan a potential defense and submitted it to the high command on August 9. Boineberg was aware of previous French plans for the defense of the city, which traditionally assumed that three corps would be needed. This level of resources was impossible given the calamity in Normandy and Boineberg trimmed the requirement to three infantry divisions, which also proved impossible. As a result, Boineberg assigned tasks to available units as an expedient. The core of the city's defense was the 325.Sicherungs (Security) Division, which had been culled to two regiments. They were assigned two of the city's three defensive sectors, Paris-Northwest, and Paris-Northeast. The Paris-St. Cloud sector was assigned to the police and security units of Feldkommandantur 758. All three sectors of the "Boineberg Line," were reinforced with Luftwaffe Flak troops from the 1.Flak Brigade along with improvised security units.

Within Paris itself, Boineberg had established a variety of defensive positions around major administrative buildings and other important points, consisting mainly of sandbagged defenses, occasional concrete defenses, and various types of roadblocks and obstructions. In addition, 32 key locations were designated as *Stützpunkte* (strongpoints), with the buildings reinforced with sandbags and other defenses, and supplies put in place to allow the position to hold out for 30 days. This included key German military posts such as the Army's Kommendatura on Place de l'Opéra, the casernes at Place de la République and Porte de la Clignancourt, the Luftwaffe headquarters in the Palais du Luxembourg, as well as major government buildings such as the, Senate, Chamber of Deputies, Foreign Affairs Ministry, the École Militaire and key hotels used as German administrative centers such as the

Meurice, Majestic, Crillon and Continental. Boineberg resisted instructions from Berlin to prepare the main Seine River bridges for demolition, fearing that this would have grave repercussions for German tactical movement without serving any useful purpose aside from Hitler's thirst for revenge. By mid-August 1944, Paris had ceased to be a major Wehrmacht administrative center, but it still remained an absolutely essential transport and communications link between Germany and the front lines, and this was a major focus in the Paris commander's planning in mid-August. On a daily basis, German units could be seen moving to the front through Paris, especially along the roadways of the Grande Ceinture, the road and rail ring around the city. Indeed, when Choltitz arrived, he quickly appreciated that the available forces were insufficient to defend the city against an Allied attack, but at a minimum he hoped to keep the roads open for the Wehrmacht as long as possible.

US PLANS

Allied planning prior to the Normandy landings presumed that Paris would be avoided as a major objective. The city was shielded to the west by the Marne and Oise rivers, which offered good defensive prospects, and the thought of prolonged street fighting dissuaded Allied planners. Instead, the presumption was that the Seine River would be crossed to the northwest and southeast of Paris, encircling the city and eventually forcing its surrender without direct combat. This remained the Allied plan through the middle of August 1944. Bradley bluntly described the US attitude after the war: "Tactically, the city had become meaningless. For all its past glories, Paris represented nothing more than an inkspot on our maps to be bypassed as we headed toward the Rhine. Logistically it could cause untold trouble, for behind its handsome facades there lived 4,000,000 hungry Frenchmen." In the cold calculus of war, Paris would require 4,000 tons of supplies per day, which was equivalent to the amount needed to push Patton's Third Army three days closer toward the German border.

The Allied advance following Operation *Cobra* was so explosive that Allied planning changed almost daily. Following the decision in early August to shift the emphasis of Patton's Third Army from a westward advance through Brittany to an eastward advance toward the Seine, his units had made remarkable progress against feeble resistance. While the bulk of the German forces fought for their lives in the Falaise pocket, Patton's forces raced eastward, largely unchecked except for occasional defenses in the major cities. During the second week of August, Haislip's XV Corps had sped around the southern flank of the German Seventh Army and established a defensive line around Argentan. With the Canadian First Army heading southward past Falaise, the German Army in Normandy now was at risk of being trapped in the Falaise–Argentan pocket. On the afternoon of August 13, Bradley ordered Haislip to halt any further advance toward the Canadians and to prepare to shift his advance back eastward toward the Seine. Bradley regarded the Falaise operation as being a hammer and anvil, with Montgomery's 21st Army Group playing the hammer role. With the American anvil in place, Bradley turned his attention to other objectives. This decision has been the subject of enormous debate since then, as some critics argue that XV Corps could have sealed the Falaise pocket sooner, thereby capturing more German troops than were bagged when the

pocket finally closed a week later on August 20. The merits of this debate are outside the scope of this book.

Allied planners considered a major airborne drop, Operation *Transfigure*, for execution on August 17 to trap retreating elements of the German Seventh Army south of Paris and facilitate Patton's advance. The US 101st Airborne Division would drop near St. Arnoult-en-Yvelines and the British 1st Airborne Division and Polish 1st Airborne Brigade near Rambouillet. By August 16, Patton's tanks had almost reached Rambouillet and so the airborne operation was postponed. It was next targeted at seizing bridgeheads over the Seine River. Once again, Patton's columns were faster, arriving on August 19 near Mantes.

By mid-August, Bradley recognized that the defensive vacuum in front of Patton's Third Army offered the opportunity for a rapid exploitation toward the Seine River. This became Patton's primary objective in the third week of August. On the northern axis, the lead elements of Haislip's XV Corps, the 5th Armored Division, had reached Dreux along the Eure River. By the time that the Falaise pocket was sealed on August 20, Haislip's corps had two divisions on the Seine River near Mantes above Paris and had begun crossing the river on August 19. Indeed, Haislip's corps had pushed so fast that they had crossed the phase lines not only of the neighboring US First Army, but into the sector assigned to Montgomery's 21st Army Group. On the center axis, Major-General Walton Walker's XX Corps was assigned the Paris–Orléans gap.

The capture of Mantes on August 19 by the 79th Infantry Division put the US Army within a short striking distance of Paris. Nevertheless, Bradley continued to regard Paris more as a potential nuisance than a potential opportunity. (NARA)

At the time, the corps' resources were meager: the 5th Infantry Division and the newly arrived 7th Armored Division. Their initial objective was the city of Chartres, which they reached by August 16. On the southern axis, Eddy's XII Corps was operating "deep in Indian country" with hardly any German forces in sight, and moving swiftly toward the Champagne region. While it might seem that Paris would have fallen under the purview of Patton's Third Army, on August 23 Bradley substantially reconfigured the 12th Army Group composition to disentangle the eastward drive. Haislip's XV Corps was shifted to First Army control, and First Army assigned the task of racing to Paris with its V Corps coming up from the rear. Patton's Third Army continued its rapid advance eastward over the Seine with its focus now south of the city. The primary constraint to all of these operations was the lack of fuel, and the 12th Army Group was forced to develop improvised means to supply the advance columns, such as the Red Ball Express truck columns and an airlift of fuel to captured airbases immediately behind the front lines.

FRENCH PLANS

While Paris played a minor role in the plans of the Wehrmacht and US Army, it was central to French strategic planning. De Gaulle viewed the liberation of Paris as essential to his main aim—to establish a new state to replace the discredited Third Republic. Beyond the humiliating defeat in 1940, Pétain's Vichy government had further degraded itself by collaboration with the Germans. Yet de Gaulle was loathed by Churchill and deeply distrusted by Roosevelt. The US State Department leaned toward an idealistic Wilsonian policy that frowned on European colonial possessions. Not only had de Gaulle based his legitimacy at first on the support of France's African colonies, but in the eyes of Washington, he was a self-appointed military ruler reminiscent of the despised tinpot autocrats of Latin America. De Gaulle's GPRF (Gouvernement Provisoire de la République Française) had no political legitimacy beyond that granted by Britain and the United States; the US granted formal recognition only on July 13, 1944. The Anglo-American alliance with France was a marriage of convenience, a lesser evil than acknowledging the evaporating legitimacy of Pétain's Vichy French government.

Eisenhower's policies had more of a realpolitik flavor than Washington's, and his autonomy gave him some freedom from the dictates of the State Department. Eisenhower's relations with de Gaulle and the French were more cordial for pragmatic reasons, recognizing the superb performance of the tough French mountain troops in the Italian campaign, and deeply appreciative of the efforts of the FFI resistance in the unfolding Brittany campaign. In December 1943, Eisenhower had assured de Gaulle that "I have no notion of entering Paris without your troops." Eisenhower was not tightly constrained by the State Department's dyspeptic view of de Gaulle, and this freedom of action would play a pivotal role in US decision-making in August 1944.

While de Gaulle would have liked to have had the entire French First Army deployed in northwest France to take part in the liberation of Paris, the US refused. It had been raised, trained, and equipped in the Mediterranean theater by the US, and it was assigned to take part in the second invasion of France on the Riviera in August 1944. In December 1943, Eisenhower agreed to the transfer one French division to the UK to take a symbolic part in the northwest France campaign, and de Gaulle obviously selected Leclerc's division.

De Gaulle hoped to establish political legitimacy by action, taking over control of liberated French towns and cities in the wake of the Allied advance. Britain and the United States originally planned to impose an AMGOT (Allied Military Government for Occupied Territory) in France. But de Gaulle installed his own government in Normandy sooner and it worked very effectively, removing the need for the US and British armies to divert resources to civil administration. The key element in de Gaulle's plans was similar assumption of power in Paris, with or without Allied approval. Leclerc's division was hardly enough to capture a major city, and de Gaulle was well aware of the likelihood of an uprising in the city.

Uprising was in the French blood, the catalyst of modern French politics since the 1789 revolution. Paris was imbued with the spirit of strikes, labor unrest and exuberant political demonstrations, and was often called the "Red Jerusalem." Indeed, one of the main concerns of both de Gaulle and the resistance leaders in France was that an uprising would break out spontaneously, with the risk that it could occur too soon while the Germans will still in total control and the Allied armies too far away to intervene readily. De Gaulle was concerned with another legacy of France's revolutionary tradition, the 1871 Paris Commune. The PCF might attempt to exploit an uprising and seize political power in Paris. De Gaulle had been careful to include the communists in his alliance and had carefully nurtured relations with Stalin. In return, the Moscow-based head of the PCF, Maurice Thorez, had assured de Gaulle that the party had no plans to take power during the liberation. Nevertheless, suspicions remained on both sides. After French troops and partisans liberated Corsica in October 1943, the PCF installed mayors in numerous towns.

The liberation of Paris was the central objective of all French leaders, whether de Gaulle's Free French, the political resistance of all stripes, and the communist-dominated FFI insurgents. (MHI)

There was considerable controversy within the resistance about the best tactical approach. The PCF and its main fighting groups such as the Francs-Tireurs et Partisans (FTP) preferred continual guerilla struggle and sabotage, the regulation Moscow approach for partisan operations. Many other groups of both the left and right did not favor armed actions until the approach of Allied forces for fear of German reprisals. The communist call for action attracted many young men on the run from compulsory labor press-gangs, regardless of their politics. The communists regularly accused the other groups of "*attentisme*," procrastination; the other groups accused the communists of being hotheaded radicals apt to precipitate a bloodbath. The communists tended to be more belligerent in word than deed, and Col. Rol's refrain that "Paris is worth 200,000 dead" was a reminder of their romanticization of violent action. In reality, the weakness of the various resistance groups in the city precluded any large-scale, armed actions until the Allies were nearby.

The FFI leadership already had reached a tentative agreement about how the seizure of power was to be undertaken. The police were likely to be the most numerous force and so would be responsible for taking over all governmental buildings and putting de Gaulle's officials in place. Non-governmental facilities were to be the responsibility of the smaller FFI contingents, who were only about a quarter the strength of the police. Some prominent public buildings such as the Hôtel de Ville were to be seized by joint forces. From the perspective of the resistance in Paris, an uprising in Paris in August 1944 was inevitable: only its timing and direction was in question. After the experience in the Haute-Savoie mountains earlier in 1944 when the resistance was crushed after attempting to create a mountain sanctuary, the Gaullists preferred the more realistic course of delaying the start of the insurrection as long as possible; Col. Rol and the communists were eager to start it as soon as possible.

OPPOSING FORCES

GERMAN ARMY

By mid-August 1944, the Wehrmacht in northern France was in retreat and on the verge of rout. The bulk of the Seventh Army and Panzergruppe West was nearly trapped around Falaise, while Fifteenth Army on the Pas de Calais had been stripped of its better units for the Normandy fighting and was left with little but its second-class static divisions, huddled in the bunkers on the Atlantic Wall coast.

In the face of retreating German units, Gen. z.b.V. AOK 1 attempted to set up blocking positions on the Loire and Seine rivers south of Paris starting on August 10. When the operations section of AOK 1 arrived in Fontainebleau, the only units actually under its direct command were the AOK 1 *Sturmbataillon*, the AOK 1 *Wach Kompanie*, and an improvised reconnaissance company with captured French vehicles and these took a few days to arrive. The 325.Sicherungs Division in Paris was ordered to shed two of its units, with Sicherungs Regiment 6 being sent to Chartres, and Sicherungs Regiment 1 positioned between Chartres and Auteuil to cover the western side of Paris. The Chartres sector was reinforced with the AOK 1 assault battalion. The

AOK 1 had very modest resources to block the Orléans gap, consisting mainly of security units with second-rate equipment. This 1940-vintage Somua S-35 tank was typical of the captured French tanks used by these units, in this case with the Panzer company of Sicherungs Regiment 101, lost while defending Montargis against the US 5th Infantry Division in August 1944. The vehicle to the right is a US Army T2 tank recovery vehicle preparing to drag the disabled German tanks off the road. (NARA)

The paucity of regular army units forced AOK 1 to rely heavily on local Luftwaffe Flak units to create a skeleton for the defense of towns along the Seine. This is an 88mm gun of Flak Abteilung 555 on the heights overlooking the Seine near Mantes where the 79th Infantry Division made its crossing. (NARA)

first of the promised reinforcements began arriving on August 13, a single regiment from the newly reformed 48.Infanterie Division, and it was directed toward Chartres. To defend the Loire–Seine sector south of Paris, Sicherungs Regiment 1010 was taken from Brigade West and sent to this area. Panzer support for these defenses was minimal: a Panhard 178 *Panzersphawagen Kompanie* with Sicherungs Regiment 6 and a Somua S-35 *Panzer Kompanie* with Sicherungs Regiment 1010, both in the Chartres sector. Some elements of the 352.Infanterie Division were withdrawing through this area and put under the control of the local commander.

The core of the German defenses in Paris was the 325.Sicherungs Division "Wach Paris" (325th "Paris Alert" Security Division) commanded by Generalmajor Brehmer. This had a nominal strength of four regiments with about 6,000 troops, though as noted above, two of the regiments were taken away by AOK 1 to help reinforce the outer defenses. This type of security division was extremely weak compared with field divisions, lacking motor transport and having only minimal field artillery. Security divisions were composed mostly of over-age soldiers with foreign small arms and were intended only for occupation duty, not front-line combat. Generalleutnant von Boineberg attempted to reinforce the division by improvised means in 1944. Sicherungs Regimenter 1 and 6 were motorized using confiscated French city buses, but as mentioned, these units were sent west to Autueil. A separate unit, Bataillon 569 of Transport Begleit Regiment—Paris had scattered guard posts along the Grande Ceinture, the rail-line encircling the city. The Front Weapons Depot at Paris-Garche had formed Panzer Abteilung 100 with old French tanks but this was committed to Normandy in the summer leaving behind a single company. Panzer Kompanie Paris was formed from 13 old tanks which included a motley assortment of Renault R-35, R-40, Hotchkiss H-39, Somua S-35 and Char B1-bis as well as a few old PzKpfw I tanks.

Besides the formal military formations, the Paris commander nominally had control over any other able-bodied troops in the city. Attempts were made through mid-August to form various Wehrmacht office workers and support staff into improvised military formations, called alert battalions P-I to P-IV (P = Paris). One of the battalions was made up of the numerous translators from the many headquarters in the city. A scheme to arm the city defenders with the potent new Panzerfaust anti-tank rocket went awry when there was an explosion at the engineer camp where the instruction was taking place, killing about 120 soldiers including much of the training staff.

The most substantial forces in the Paris area aside from the 325.Sicherungs Division were the Flak units of Luftwaffe's 1.Flak Brigade, mainly protecting industrial areas and railroads around Paris. This consisted of three regiments with about two dozen Flak battalions totaling over 36 heavy and 220 medium/light flak guns. These were a mixture of configurations including seven railroad Flak battalions, 12 semi-mobile battalions and four fixed battalions; of these six were heavy 88mm battalions, seven were mixed 20mm–37mm battalions and 10 were light 20mm battalions. Besides this brigade, the three battalions of Fallschirmjäger Flak Regiment 11 were protecting the airbases at Villacoublay, Brétigny and Villaroche in the southern suburbs. Boineberg was able to cajole the Luftwaffe command to shed some weapons to establish defenses along major roads leading into the city.

Besides the Flak units, the Luftwaffe had 13 major airbases around the city, and in most cases these bases had their own Luftwaffe defense companies, which were sometimes combined with local Flak units to create improvised defense groups. Luftwaffe air units in the Paris area had grown extremely weak owing to continual Allied air attacks on the airfields and heavy attrition from the summer air battles. The end came on August 17 when the Luftwaffe was ordered to destroy the airfields in the Paris area. Luftflotte 3 was moved from Paris to Reims, the two remaining fighter groups were withdrawn, and fighter operations were turned over to units farther from the Seine. By the third week of August, the Luftwaffe was down to only 16 fighter groups in all of France and had less than 150 fighters serviceable. The attrition along the Seine was murderous because of the inexperience of the new fighter crews. On August 18 alone, five fighters were shot down plus another 27 missing and presumed lost. As the Luftwaffe pulled out of the Paris area, some of the Flak and Luftwaffe ground defense units retreated with the squadrons.

By the third week of August, Choltitz had a nominal force of about 20,000 troops of which about 5,000 were attached to the 325.Sicherungs Division inside the city and the remainder in various units scattered around the city. Choltitz was also authorized to commandeer any units passing through the city, and managed to appropriate a relief column of about a dozen Panther tanks, probably intended for the Panzer Lehr Division.

The city was divided into three sectors with their own field commands, FK Nordwest, FK Ost, and FK St. Cloud; the first two commands were based on the two remaining regiments of the 325.Sicherungs Division. The exterior sector centered on St. Cloud was assigned to the former Feldkommandantur 758 (FK 758), which consisted of four security battalions and six military police detachments. The security battalions like those in Paris were made up of over-age troops equipped with captured weapons. The military police units on the other hand were well organized, well trained and had ample vehicles and motorcycles. However, the units were widely scattered and the MP units were deployed in modest 30-man detachments since the unit covered a wide area including Versailles, Rambouillet, Corbeil and Mantes.

Such modest forces were barely able to contain the increasingly active French resistance movement inside the city, and were completely inadequate to offer any serious defense against the onrushing Allied forces. Hitler's nihilistic instructions to destroy the city were equally unrealistic given the lack of engineers or ample supplies of demolitions. The AOK 1 headquarters bluntly assessed the combat potential of the Paris garrison: "In view of the peculiar difficulties of fighting in large cities and the material superiority of the enemy, any real resistance on the part of the Paris military district could not be expected."

WEHRMACHT UNITS, GREATER PARIS AREA, AUGUST 1944

Kommandant Festung Paris	General der Infanterie Dietrich von Choltitz
Feldkommandantur Paris—Nordwest	Oberst Hans Jay
Feldkommandantur Paris—Ost	Oberst Krause
Feldkommandantur Paris—St. Cloud (FK 758)	Oberst Kurt Hesse

ARMY (HEER) UNITS

325.Sicherungs Division	Generalmajor Walter Brehmer
Sicherungs Regiment 1*	Oberst Kurt von Kräwel
Sicherungs Regiment 5	Oberst Werner Friemel
Sicherungs Regiment 6*	Oberstleutnant Wilhelm Stier
Sicherungs Regiment 190	Oberst Garbsch
Transport Begleit Regiment—Paris	Oberstleutnant Hauk

LUFTWAFFE UNITS

1.Flak Brigade	Oberst Egon Baur
Flak Regiment 59 (v)** (11 battalions)	Oberst von Bose
Flak Regiment 100 (mot) (11 battalions)	Oberst Max Kriesche
Flak Regiment 114 (o) (1 battalion)	Oberst Conrad Büchner
Fallschirmjäger Flak Regiment 11	Oberst Karl Meise

*deployed to Chartres after August 15, 1944

**(v) Verlegefähigen, semi-mobile; (mot), motorized; (o) Ortsfesten, fixed

US ARMY

The US Army units approaching Paris consisted of three corps from Patton's Third Army. To the north, Haislip's XV Corps had diverted northward away from Paris, heading for a Seine crossing well north of the city. This corps had penetrated deeper than any Allied unit and was largely unopposed once it had raced past Dreux. To its south, Walker's XX Corps had encountered the only major defenses in its path around Chartres on August 16: the battlegroup of AOK 1. Once these defenses were overcome, XX Corps continued pushing eastward toward the Seine south of Paris. XII Corps had emerged from the Loire Valley and was heading toward Troyes.

These corps tended to be relatively light at this stage of the war, based around an infantry and armored division. An absolutely vital ingredient in each corps was the attachment of a mechanized cavalry group or separate mechanized cavalry squadrons. In such fluid battlefield conditions, these reconnaissance units played a vital role in both scouting and flank security.

LEFT
The fast pace of the race to the Seine put a premium on mechanized cavalry to scout ahead of the main force and protect extended and unprotected flanks. Here, an M8 light armored car of the 87th Cavalry Reconnaissance Squadron, engages a German ambush near Epernay, on August 27 after the 7th Armored Division had pushed out of the Melun bridgehead on the Seine. (NARA)

BELOW LEFT
Most of the river crossings in the final weeks of August were by improvised means using local boats or engineer rafts. Here a squad from the 80th Infantry Division crosses the Meuse on September 1 near St. Mihiel. (NARA)

Each corps typically had an attached artillery group with five to seven artillery battalions equipped with a mixture of 105mm howitzers, 155mm howitzers and 155mm guns. The corps also had an attached engineer combat group, typically consisting of about five engineer battalions with a mixture of combat engineer and bridging units. Combat bridging battalions were absolutely vital to keeping the corps moving over the numerous rivers as, by this stage of the war, most bridges had been destroyed by either Allied airpower or retreating German units.

The FFI was active in the Oise region in front of Paris, coordinated by British Special Operations Executive (SOE) and US Office of Strategic Services (OSS) teams. The FFI detachments were not strong enough to confront German combat units, but as a later report noted, "like termites they caused the whole German edifice to crumble." They were a major impediment to

A key ingredient in rapid offensive operations was the provision of ample combat engineering assets for rapid breaching of river obstacles. Here, a treadway bridge is completed at Vulaines-sur-Seine near Fontainebleau on August 24 to assist in the crossing of the 5th Infantry Division. (NARA)

German transit in the combat zone, and their harassment helped to demoralize the German garrison and speed their evacuation in August 1944. The FFI was also instrumental in providing reconnaissance and intelligence to Patton's Third Army and were deeply appreciated by US units for their service.

The main problem facing Patton's Third Army in the third week of August was logistics rather than the German defenses. Ammunition stocks were still ample as German resistance had been so feeble. However, the fast-moving columns were running out of fuel and food. Bradley was extremely frustrated by the decision of SHAEF to reserve most of the available airlift for Operation *Transfigure*, and this didn't become available until after August 19 when *Transfigure* was finally rendered moot by operations on the ground. Starting on August 19, transport aircraft became available to airlift fuel and food and Patton's widely dispersed columns.

THIRD ARMY (-)*	LIEUTENANT-GENERAL GEORGE S. PATTON
182nd Field Artillery Group	Colonel N. McMahon
1117th Engineer Combat Group	Colonel R. Lovett
XV Corps**	Major-General Wade Haislip
5th Armored Division	Major-General Jack Heard
79th Division	Major-General Ira Wyche
XX Corps	Major-General Walton Walker
7th Armored Division	Major-General Lindsay Silvester
30th Division	Major-General Leland Hobbs
XII Corps	Major-General Manton Eddy***
4th Armored Division	Major-General John Wood
35th Division	Major-General Paul Baade

*VIII Corps still in Brittany through August 1944

**Transferred to Hodges' First Army on August 23, 1944

***Eddy replaced Major-General Gilbert Cook on August 21

Ultimately, it was the First Army's V Corps sent to Paris rather than Patton's Third Army. The two main units deployed were the US 4th Infantry Division, and Leclerc's 2e Division Blindée (2e DB). The corps also had the 5th Armored Division and 28th Infantry Division attached at this time but merely on paper: the 28th Division was in a blocking position on the Eure River in XIX Corps' sector and the 5th Armored Division was on the Seine river in XV Corps' sector. The V Corps had a substantial amount of supporting elements including a cavalry group with two squadrons; three field artillery groups with 14 artillery battalions; two engineer groups with five battalions; one armored group with five separate tank battalions; one tank destroyer group with seven tank destroyer battalions, plus other supporting elements.

The 4th Infantry Division landed on Utah Beach on D-Day and had fought continuously since then. From D-Day through August 1, its casualties had totaled 10,396 including 1,844 killed and 7,019 wounded out of an authorized strength of 14,235 men. This was the second highest casualty tally in the US Army in Normandy next to the 29th Division which had landed on Omaha Beach. These casualties fell most heavily on the soldiers in the rifle platoons. So, for example, the 22nd Infantry Regiment had suffered 1,814 casualties among the 2,513 men who landed on Utah Beach and totaled 3,439 casualties through August 1 when replacements are counted, in other words 136 percent casualties in about two months of fighting. By August 1944, the 4th Infantry Division was an experienced and well-trained division and its casualties were continually replaced to keep it at or near full strength.

FRENCH ARMY

Leclerc's 2e Division Blindée had been raised near Rabat, Morocco, starting in August 1943, and patterned on the standard US Army armored division. The core element of the division was the troops of Leclerc's Force L with the unit filled out with volunteers from France's North African colonies as well as volunteers and troops who had escaped to England after 1940. Although based on American tables of organization, the component battalions retained their French regimental lineage so the three tank battalions were the

The 2e Division Blindée came ashore at Utah Beach on August 1, and was thrown into the fighting around Argentan on August 10 against the 9.Panzer Division. Here, a T2 tank recovery vehicle of the 1/RMT comes ashore from a US Navy LCT. (NARA)

The 2e Division Blindée was organized and equipped like a US Army armored division, but kept its French unit designations. This is an M3A3 light tank named "Vexin" of 12e RCA, one of the division's three tank battalions. (NARA)

501e Régiment de Chars de Combat (RCC), the 12e Régiment de Chasseurs d'Afrique (RCA) and the 12e Régiment de Cuirassiers. The 501e RCC was based around the 342e Compagnie de Chars, a separate company of Hotchkiss light tanks that had served in the Norwegian campaign in 1940, moved to England after that campaign, and then took part in Leclerc's legendary campaign in Equatorial Africa with or without tanks. The 12e RCA had earlier taken part on the Allied side during the fighting around Kasserine Pass, equipped with Somua S-35 cavalry tanks. A cadre from this regiment was used to reconstitute the 12e Régiment de Cuirassiers in August 1943. The three mechanized infantry battalions originally derived from the Régiment de Tirailleurs Sénégalais du Tchad (Senegalese Rifle Regiment of Chad) which was renamed as the Régiment de Marche de Tchad (RMT) when it was decided against using black African troops in the division in favor of French and Spanish volunteers. Perhaps the most unusual formation in the division was the Régiment Blindé de Fusiliers Marins (RBFM). This unit was formed from French naval infantry units based in Bizerte and Toulon who volunteered for the Free French forces after the Vichy French fleet was scuttled in November 1942. They served as the personnel for the division's tank destroyer battalion and retained bits of their distinctive naval garb through the 1944 fighting. Another difference between the US and French pattern was the naming of the division's three combat commands. Instead of the American practices of letters (CCA, CCB, CCR), the 2e DB's *groupements tactiques* were lettered after their commanders (GTD, GTL, GTV).

The 2e DB was transferred from Morocco to England in April 1944, and landed in Normandy in July 1944. It was attached to Haislip's XV Corps and entered combat on August 10, 1944, attacking the 9.Panzer Division in the Écouves Forest on the approaches to Argentan during the attempts to seal the Falaise pocket.

V CORPS — MAJOR-GENERAL LEONARD GEROW

4th Infantry Division	Major-General Raymond Barton
8th Infantry Regiment	Colonel James Rodwell
12th Infantry Regiment	Colonel James Luckett
22nd Infantry Regiment	Colonel Charles Lanham
20th Field Artillery Battalion (155mm)	
29th Field Artillery Battalion (105mm)	
42nd Field Artillery Battalion (105mm)	
44th Field Artillery Battalion (105mm)	
70th Tank Battalion*	
801st Tank Destroyer Battalion*	
2e Division Blindée	Général Jacques Leclerc
Groupement Tactique D (GTD)	Colonel Louis Dio
12e Régiment de Cuirassiers	
1/Régiment de Marche de Tchad	
3e Régiment d'Artillerie Coloniale	
Groupement Tactique L (GTL)	Colonel Paul Girod de Langlade
12e Régiment de Chasseurs d'Afrique	
2/Régiment de Marche de Tchad	
40e Régiment d'Artillerie Nord Africaine	
Groupement Tactique V (GTV)	Colonel Louis Warabiot until August 8, then Colonel Paul Bilotte
501e Régiment de Chars de Combat	
3/Régiment de Marche de Tchad	
64e Régiment d'Artillerie de la Division Blindée	

*non-divisional attachments

The 2e DB had an eclectic mix of units, none more unexpected than the naval troops of the RBFM, the division's tank destroyer battalion, who wore naval insignia and caps with their army uniforms. This is Ensign Philippe de Gaulle, son of Charles de Gaulle and adjutant in the 1/3e Escadron. (NARA)

The British SOE focused its arms supplies to FFI resistance groups outside Paris like this unit from Caen, while Paris resistance organizations were more often supplied with money and radios. (NARA)

This fighter with an FFI group in Chartres poses with a German submachine gun. Most women in the French resistance served in the less romantic and more dangerous roles of intelligence agents and couriers. (NARA)

FRENCH RESISTANCE

French resistance organizations sprang up autonomously after the 1940 defeat and de Gaulle attempted to bring them under a unified organization in 1942–43. The armed resistance groups grew substantially in 1942–43 following the disbandment of the Vichy French army in November 1942 and the German imposition of a forced labor law in February 1943. De Gaulle attempted to exert control over the resistance through the BCRA (Bureau Central de Reseignements et d'Action: Central Intelligence and Action Bureau), the intelligence arm of the Free French forces. The BCRA was able to influence the resistance groups by directing supplies of money, weapons and equipment to them. The most important of the political unification efforts in occupied France was the formation in May 1943 of the National Council of the Resistance (CNR: Conseil National de la Résistance), which was a coalition of the five main political parties, two of the large trade union movements and more than a dozen resistance groups. In practice, it was impossible for either the BCRA or CNR to impose centralized control over this movement since by their very nature the groups had to be highly secretive to prevent penetration and destruction by the German police and their French henchmen, the Milice. In 1944, the CNR created a military command for the armed resistance groups, the Commission d'Action Militaire (COMAC: Military Action Committee). Owing to the strength of the communist FTP militia (Francs-Tireurs et Partisans) in the Paris area, COMAC appointed a communist, Col. Rol as the regional Île-de-France commander. When the Seine department commander was arrested in June 1944, Rol attempted to appoint another communist to the position but after protests from the other groups, a retired officer, Colonel Lizé-Malleret was given the position.

The FFI in the Seine department was divided into four sectors (north, south, east, west) plus a reserve, and numbered 35,523 according to the last weekly report prior to the insurrection. However, the Paris resistance groups were chronically short of weapons as the Allies were not planning military operations in Paris and so the British SOE and US OSS had parachuted few weapons into the areas around the city. The primary SOE support of the FFI in Paris was in terms of money and radios. In August 1944, the FFI reported its weaponry in the Seine department to include only 1,560 small arms: four machine guns, 83 light machine guns, 83 automatic rifles, 570 rifles, 820 revolvers and 192 grenades, hardly one weapon for every 20 insurgents. However, many militias underreported their weaponry and the actual total was perhaps three times as high. However, this still indicates that the FFI was substantially inferior in firepower to the German garrison. The best-armed militia, the communist FTP and its immediate allies, could deploy only 600 armed insurgents at the beginning of the insurrection. The shortage of weapons forced the FFI to look elsewhere for armed support, especially the Paris police. There were about 20,000 policemen in the department at the time of the insurrection, a substantial force compared to the FFI. The resistance leadership approached various police officials in the summer to convince them to support any insurrectionary movement. The police clearly understood that after liberation they could be charged with collaboration during the occupation, so there was some incentive to side with the resistance once the fighting began. But the police were equally aware that the Germans would respond brutally to any such shift of allegiance, and so timing became critical. The FFI was confident enough of police intentions that the battle plan for the insurrection assumed police participation.

THE CAMPAIGN

RACE FOR THE SEINE

By August 15, Patton's three corps were on their way toward Dreux (XV Corps), Chartres (XX Corps) and Orléans (XII Corps). The aim was to reach the Seine River and establish what was called the "D-Day lodgement area," the section of northwest France up to the Seine River that would be the base for further Allied operations in the autumn and winter of 1944 on the approaches to Germany. There were no orders to cross the Seine River, only to clear the western bank.

Haislip's XV Corps encountered modest resistance, as the German Seventh Army was preoccupied trying to fight their way out of the Falaise gap. The 79th Infantry Division had been motorized starting on August 14 to keep pace with the neighboring 5th Armored Division and was reinforced with the 749th Tank Battalion and 813th Tank Destroyer Battalion. To facilitate a rapid advance, the 106th Cavalry Group spearheaded it. The 79th Division moved toward Nogent-le-Roi while the 5th Armored Division moved on Dreux. Both divisions crossed the Eure River on August 16, and the 5th Armored Division took Dreux against modest resistance by that afternoon. The German defenses in Dreux were typical of this sector, about 700 troops

Chartres was finally cleared of German troops on August 19 by the 11th Infantry Regiment, 5th Infantry Division, which dislodged the Luftwaffe Flak school from the southeast corner of the city. (NARA)

Chartres was one of the few citys stoutly defended by AOK 1. The US attack was hamstrung by an unwillingness to employ heavy artillery fire for fear of damaging the famous cathedral, seen here with troops of the 11th Infantry Regiment in the foreground. (NARA)

of the AOK 7 *Sturmbataillon*, some troops of the 352.Infanterie Division and various police and security units. Most of the tank casualties suffered that day by the 5th Armored Division were to the 88mm anti-aircraft guns of Flak Abteilung 555 near the town. The 79th Infantry Division encountered less resistance, a strafing attack in which the Luftwaffe lost three fighters to divisional anti-aircraft machine guns. On August 15, the division was instructed to secure the heights overlooking the Seine River at Mantes-Gassicourt. The 79th Infantry Division established a bridgehead over the Eure on the afternoon of August 16, placing it only 37 miles (60km) from Paris. The division pushed forward toward the town and the 314th Infantry Regiment began entering it on August 19, finding the bridges in the area destroyed either by Allied air attack or German demolitions. In the meantime, the 313th Infantry Regiment to the west had moved past one of the bends in the Seine River where they found a catwalk over a dam. Since the mission was simply to hold the left bank of the Seine, the regiment was ordered to destroy the catwalk. The regimental commander took his time executing the order since he had sent a platoon across and didn't have enough explosives for such a mission. In the meantime, Patton had visited the divisional headquarters and had taken the opportunity to looking at the area for future crossing sites.

The timing of the unauthorized crossing was fortuitous. That day, Eisenhower had met with Montgomery and Bradley to discuss operational planning. The original D-Day plans had not expected Allied forces to reach the outer boundary of the D-Day lodgment area, until D+90, when in fact it had been reached on D+74. This had created significant logistics challenges that slowed the advance of Patton's Third Army. All three commanders agreed to ignore earlier plans and to exploit the current German predicament. As part of this issue, Bradley raised the problem posed by Haislip's intrusion into the British 21st Army Group sector near Mantes. Bradley offered to provide Montgomery with trucks to substitute British forces at Mantes, but Montgomery declined owing to his focus on the Falaise operation. Montgomery had long been a proponent of a long envelopment on the Seine, which might trap as many as 75,000 German troops on the left bank. As a result, Montgomery encouraged Bradley to ignore the inter-Allied boundaries and exploit the opportunity. Bradley contacted Patton and authorized him to begin a crossing operation that his staff had already begun to study that afternoon.

That evening, Patton ordered Major-General Wyche of the 79th Infantry Division to begin crossing the Seine. The order to blow the dam was rescinded and the 313th Infantry Regiment was instructed to establish a bridgehead on the right bank of the Seine. The 314th Infantry Regiment likewise began crossing the Seine at Mantes, at first by improvised means and subsequently by organized ferries. The 5th Armored Division provided a treadway bridge, which was established near Rosny-sur-Seine to permit the 315th to cross on

The strategic situation: August 16, 1944

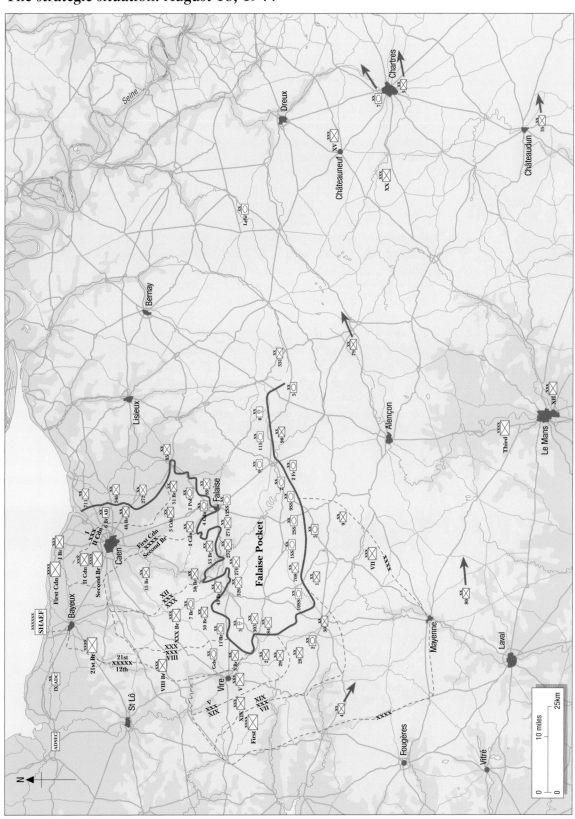

August 20. The unexpected attack surprised Model's Army Group B headquarters at the underground bunker complex at Roche-Guyon, and they hurriedly evacuated the site for Soissons. Model quickly appreciated the threat posed by the bridgehead but, lacking ground forces, attempted to stop its expansion with heavy air attacks. In one of the largest shows of strength that month, several Luftwaffe squadrons began incessant air attacks using strafing, bombs and rockets to stifle the bridgehead. In response, XV Corps moved all available anti-aircraft defenses around the bridge, beginning with 40mm Bofors and quad .50-cal. machine guns, but eventually including 90mm guns. Starting with the heavy raids of August 21, the US anti-aircraft gunners claimed about 50 aircraft shot down in four days of fighting; the actual total was about half. The Luftwaffe attacks failed to inflict significant damage on any of the bridges and, starting on August 22, the 18.Luftwaffe Felddivision arrived in the Mantes sector and began counterattacks.

The advance by Walker's XX Corps encountered the only significant German resistance in Patton's advance at Chartres. The defense was initially constituted as Kampfgruppe Garbsch and based on Sicherungs Regiment 6 from Paris, the local Sicherungs Regiment 195 of FK 751, a Luftwaffe Flak training center, Feld Flak Schule 31 West, along with Flak Bataillone 623 and 959. The Flak school was transformed into a mixed Flak regiment a few days before the fighting and included three heavy batteries with 10 88mm and three 105mm guns, as well as three mixed batteries with quad 20mm and 37mm automatic cannon, plus several more batteries of 20mm automatic cannon from the two other battalions. The city had been designated as an absorption point to collect stragglers withdrawing east, and the local commander took control of elements of the 352.Infanterie Division and scattered companies from several other divisions. The Chartres defenses were stiffened by a motley selection of tanks including a company of Somua S-35 tanks under Sicherungs Regiment 1010 outside the city, five Kingtiger heavy tanks of Panzer Kompanie (Fkl) 316 around Châteaudun, about six Hotchkiss H-39s with security units in the city, and elements of Panzer Regiment 15, 11.Panzer

An M4 tank of the 81st Tank Battalion, 5th Armored Division, passes by an abandoned 75mm Pak 40 anti-tank gun during the fighting for Dreux on August 16. (NARA)

Division, with about a dozen PzKpfw IV tanks which arrived on the southern route toward Chartres shortly before the battle for the city.

Coincidentally, the AOK 1 sector headquarters held a meeting in Chartres on August 15 owing to to the arrival of the army commander, General der Infanterie Kurt von der Chevallerie, to plan the disposition of other units ordered to the area. The first reinforcements to arrive included a regiment from the 338.Infanterie Division from southern France, and subsequently artillery elements of the 708.Infanterie Division and a regiment from the 48.Infanterie Division. Neither side expected a major encounter that day when lead elements of the 7th Armored Division began probing into the outskirts of the city. Chevallerie appointed the commander of the 48.Infanterie Division, Generalleutnant Karl Casper, to command the Chartres defense, taking over from Oberst Garbsch.

The 7th Armored Division had arrived in Normandy on August 10–14, and began a hurried road march east. The defenses to the southeast of the city were weak and on August 15, the 7th Armored Division's combat command overran these along the Eure river. Their CCA pushed through Kampfgruppe Weber, consisting mostly of Flak batteries, near Senonches, while CCR and CCA overwhelmed Kampfgruppe Kräwel from Sicherungs Regiment 1 at La Loupe and Courville. As it became evident on August 15 that Chartres was defended, the division prepared an assault for August 16; the size of the defense force was seriously underestimated at about 800 troops when it in fact was 3,500 and growing. Combat Command A (CCA) skirted the city to

Orléans fell on August 16 to an improvised task force based on mixed elements of the 4th Armored Division and the 35th Infantry Division. Here, an M10 tank destroyer fires on German troops on the opposite bank of the Loire River with the cathedral evident in the background. (NARA)

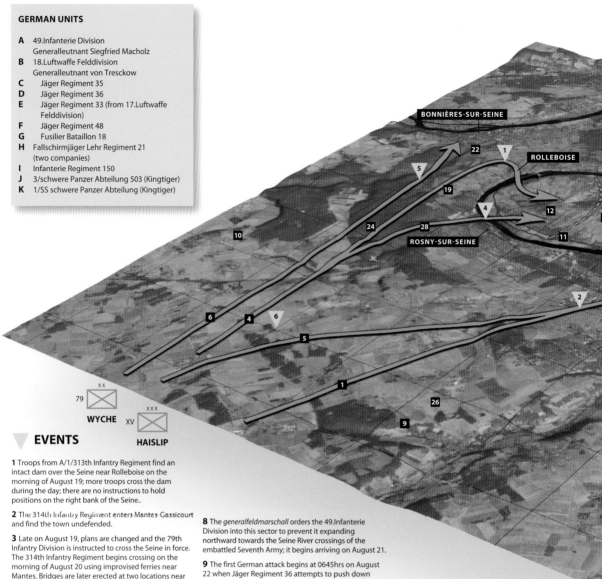

GERMAN UNITS

A 49.Infanterie Division
   Generalleutnant Siegfried Macholz
B 18.Luftwaffe Felddivision
   Generalleutnant von Tresckow
C Jäger Regiment 35
D Jäger Regiment 36
E Jäger Regiment 33 (from 17.Luftwaffe
   Felddivision)
F Jäger Regiment 48
G Fusilier Bataillon 18
H Fallschirmjäger Lehr Regiment 21
   (two companies)
I Infanterie Regiment 150
J 3/schwere Panzer Abteilung 503 (Kingtiger)
K 1/SS schwere Panzer Abteilung (Kingtiger)

BONNIÈRES-SUR-SEINE

ROLLEBOISE

ROSNY-SUR-SEINE

79 **WYCHE**
XV **HAISLIP**

▼ EVENTS

1 Troops from A/1/313th Infantry Regiment find an intact dam over the Seine near Rolleboise on the morning of August 19; more troops cross the dam during the day; there are no instructions to hold positions on the right bank of the Seine..

2 The 314th Infantry Regiment enters Mantes-Gassicourt and find the town undefended.

3 Late on August 19, plans are changed and the 79th Infantry Division is instructed to cross the Seine in force. The 314th Infantry Regiment begins crossing on the morning of August 20 using improvised ferries near Mantes. Bridges are later erected at two locations near the town, and two battalions of the 315th Infantry Regiment cross on August 20

4 The 313th Infantry Regiment crosses using ferries near Rosny-sur-Seine as well as over the dam. The XV Corps engineers later build a 40-ton treadway bridge, 565ft long at Rosny-sur-Seine.

5 The 3/315th Infantry Regiment moves forward to take up the division's left shoulder at Bonnières-sur-Seine

6 To fend off any German attacks, the corps moves up additional field artillery, with some 10 battalions and 120 howitzers eventually being deployed in support of the 79th Infantry Division.

7 The first German attack in this sector takes place on August 21 when a small *Kampfgruppe* based around the 12.Kompanie of Fallschirmjäger Lehr Regiment 21 with about 200 men and assorted vehicles makes a foray down Route 190, running into 3/314th Infantry Regiment. The skirmish lasts until late afternoon when the Germans paratroopers retreat.

8 The *generalfeldmarschall* orders the 49.Infanterie Division into this sector to prevent it expanding northward towards the Seine River crossings of the embattled Seventh Army; it begins arriving on August 21.

9 The first German attack begins at 0645hrs on August 22 when Jäger Regiment 36 attempts to push down the Fontenay–Limay road, but attack is broken up by a platoon of tanks from the 749th Tank Battalion.

10 Reports from French civilians on August 22 prompt the 313rd Infantry Regiment to send a small task force under Lieutenant-Colonel Edwin von Bibber from Vetheuil around the river bend to La Roche-Guyon to check on German reinforcements. They encounter the lead elements of the 49.Infanterie Division as well as an Army Group B Flak battalion and eventually withdraw.

11 The main attack on August 22 is delayed from 1100hrs to 2030hrs while Jäger Regiment 33 awaits reinforcements from a company of Kingtiger tanks of schwere Panzer Abteilung 503 and a company from Jäger Regiment 48 from Issou toward Limay.

12 The German attacks resume around 0615hrs on August 23. Jäger Regiment 33 is preceded by four Kingtiger tanks and Jäger Regiment 36 with six more. The attack is accompanied around 0855hrs by an air attack by 28 Fw-190 fighters of JG 2 and 11 firing rockets. Co. I/314th Infantry is pushed back, but

Lieutenant Albert Alop improvises a task force using his battery of towed quad .50-cal. anti-aircraft machine guns, an infantry platoon and some M10 tank destroyers which stop the German attack. The fighting continues through the day with the German regiments suffering 50 percent casualties due to the heavy US artillery fire: some 10 battalions with 120 howitzers.

13 The German attacks on August 24 shift to the zone of the 313th Infantry Regiment with attacks being conducted primarily by Jäger Regiment 35, which makes some penetrations before being pushed back by the afternoon.

14 After a day of relative calm, the German attack again on August 26 along the front reinforced by a second Kingtiger company, with especially heavy fighting around Fontenay. The US front held, and this is the last major German attack before the US Army goes over to the offensive.

THE SEINE BRIDGEHEAD AT MANTES: AUGUST 19–23, 1944

The US 79th Division forces a river crossing

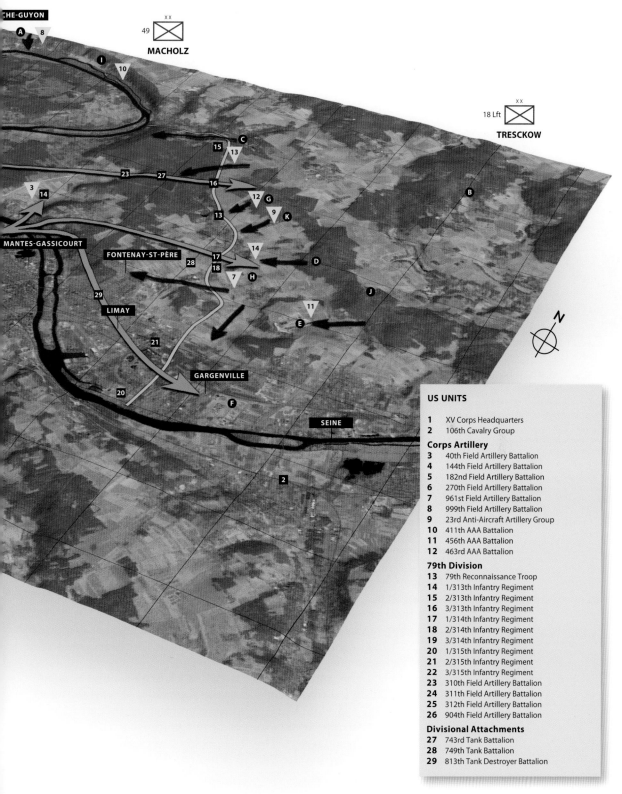

Note: Gridlines are shown at intervals of 1.24 miles/2km

HE-GUYON

49 ⊠ xx
MACHOLZ

18 Lft ⊠ xx
TRESCKOW

MANTES-GASSICOURT

FONTENAY-ST-PÈRE

LIMAY

GARGENVILLE

SEINE

N

US UNITS

1   XV Corps Headquarters
2   106th Cavalry Group

Corps Artillery

3   40th Field Artillery Battalion
4   144th Field Artillery Battalion
5   182nd Field Artillery Battalion
6   270th Field Artillery Battalion
7   961st Field Artillery Battalion
8   999th Field Artillery Battalion
9   23rd Anti-Aircraft Artillery Group
10   411th AAA Battalion
11   456th AAA Battalion
12   463rd AAA Battalion

79th Division

13   79th Reconnaissance Troop
14   1/313th Infantry Regiment
15   2/313th Infantry Regiment
16   3/313th Infantry Regiment
17   1/314th Infantry Regiment
18   2/314th Infantry Regiment
19   3/314th Infantry Regiment
20   1/315th Infantry Regiment
21   2/315th Infantry Regiment
22   3/315th Infantry Regiment
23   310th Field Artillery Battalion
24   311th Field Artillery Battalion
25   312th Field Artillery Battalion
26   904th Field Artillery Battalion

Divisional Attachments

27   743rd Tank Battalion
28   749th Tank Battalion
29   813th Tank Destroyer Battalion

Vehicles were first moved over the Seine near Mantes using improvised ferries, like these jeeps being moved across on August 20 between Gassicourt and Dennemont. (NARA)

the northeast, while CCB was directed into the city. The CCB attack was divided into two task forces, Task Force Allison (TF1) based on the 23rd Armored Infantry Battalion assigned to the northern part of the city and TF Erlenbusch (TF2) based on the 31st Tank Battalion to the southwest around the railroad station. A separate task force based around the 38th Armored Infantry Battalion from CCR was assigned the area around the airport. The fighting for the city took two days, with the 7th Armored Division constrained from using heavy artillery support because of concerns about damaging the city's legendary cathedral. The 11th Infantry Regiment from the 5th Infantry Division was brought in to provide more riflemen, and the town was secured by a final assault on the morning of August 19 with 2,000 prisoners being taken.

During the fighting for Chartres, AOK 1 tried hastily to construct a defensive line from Nemours to Giens using the rest of the 48.Infanterie Division. AOK 1 was also allotted two new Waffen-SS "Panzer divisions" though these proved to be little more than a fantasy. On August 10, the 49. and 51.Panzergrenadier brigades had been grandly re-designated as the 26. and 27.SS-Panzer divisions. In fact, the 26. was little more than a reinforced infantry regiment and the 27. was barely a regiment in strength, and their troops nothing more than personnel from schools with no unit training. They were transferred from Denmark to the Nangis–Provins area arriving after August 18, and AOK 1 attempted to reconstruct the shattered 17.SS-Panzergrenadier Division by attaching these two units to surviving elements of the divisional headquarters. This defense line never coalesced owing to the fast pace of the advance of the 7th Armored Division beyond Chartres starting on August 18.

Delayed by the defense of Chartres, Walker's XX Corps reached the Seine on August 22–23 with the 3rd Cavalry Group in the vanguard. The 7th Armored Division found the main route blocked by a heavy concentration of German artillery on the heights around Melun, mainly the 48.Infanterie Division's artillery reinforced with local Flak units. Nevertheless, there were numerous small crossings using boats and other improvised means. The 5th Infantry Division reached the heights overlooking Fontainebleau in the early hours of August 23 and rushed the river at dawn. A second crossing was made to the east at Montereau against the remnants of the 48.Infanterie Division. By the end of the day, XX Corps had five bridgeheads over the river, and corps engineers began constructing four treadway bridges. This permitted

ROCKET ATTACK ON THE SEINE BRIDGEHEAD: AUGUST 22, 1944 (pp. 44–45)

With so few resources on the ground, the Germans turned to the Luftwaffe to smash the bridgeheads over the Seine. This shows the air attack on the pontoon bridges (1) over the Seine River near Mantes on August 22, 1944, by elements of Jagdgeschwader 26. This was one of the heaviest days of fighting over the Mantes–Gassicourt bridgehead, with well over 100 German sorties. The weather was varied, with frequent periods of low cloud cover and rain. This gave the Luftwaffe some cover against Allied fighters, but it meant that the attacks frequently had to be pressed home under the clouds at altitudes below 3,000ft.

The preferred weapon for these attacks was rockets. The rocket used was the 21cm Wurfgrenate 42 Spreng (2), which was a simple adaptation of the army's Nebelwerfer artillery rocket. The rockets gave the German fighters a bit of stand-off range as they had a maximum range of six miles (9km), though they were usually launched closer to the target if the pilot wished any degree of accuracy. The rockets relied on spin-stabilization, and through the course of numerous attacks on the bridges, there were no known hits. The Luftwaffe had begun experimenting with a simple aircraft-launched version of this rocket in 1943 as a means to attack US B-17 bomber formations without having to weather their terrific defensive machine-gun fire. The launcher consisted of a pair of simple *Ofenrohre* (open tubes) suspended below the wings, and nicknamed the "Dodel." They packed a 41kg high explosive warhead and weighed 110kg on launch of which 18.4kg was solid rocket propellant. They saw their most extensive use with JG 1 and JG 26 in the autumn of 1943, usually mounted on the Focke-Wulf FW-190 A-6/R-6 as seen here (3),

but also on the Bf-109G. They were not entirely popular with the fighter squadrons in 1944, as they degraded the performance of the fighter, an especially dangerous situation in the summer of 1944 with large numbers of Allied fighters around. In the case of the bridge attacks, they were a more suitable weapon than bombs or strafing, and their bases were near enough that external fuel tanks could be dispensed with for the attacks.

Both JG 1 and JG 26 took part in rocket attacks that day, along with several neighboring Me-109 squadrons. Typically, the Me-109Gs would escort the heavily laden FW-190s into the target area as is seen here with aircraft overhead to provide some top-cover in the event of Allied fighters. After escorting the fighter-bombers, the Me-109G would sometimes then engage in strafing the bridgehead, in some cases as low as 30ft off the ground. The attacks continued until dusk, which in late summer was around 2045hrs. Among the JG 26 losses that day was Uffz. Hans Sandoz, flying "Black 4." (4)

The major anti-aircraft weapons in the bridgehead were 40mm M1 automatic cannons, the US version of the famous Bofors gun, and the M51, a towed quadruple .50-cal. heavy machine gun. By the end of the day, the two US anti-aircraft battalions in the bridgehead claimed 29 fighters shot down, 13 by the 463rd AAA and 15 by the 456th AAA although Luftwaffe records would suggest a lower total, with 23 aircraft lost on August 22, some of which in areas away from the Mantes bridgehead. A detailed account of this air battle can be found in the French military history journal *39–45* by Bruno Renoult, "Luftwaffe contre Anti-Aircraft: Les combat aériens sur la tête de pont de Mantes-août 1944" in No. 193, September 2002.

exploitation out of the bridgeheads the following day, speeded along by the extensive use of captured German trucks and other vehicles, prompting some wags to dub Walker's force the "20th Panzer Korps."

Farther south, Cook's XII Corps served primarily as a flanking force through the Loire Valley. Its main opposition came from "Gruppe Gen. z.b.V. AOK 1," a hodgepodge formation based around a regiment from the 338.Infanterie Division, four replacement battalions and some artillery from the 708.Infanterie Division. Patton was concerned that the Germans might push units up from the south against the undefended American southern flank, and XII Corps' mission was largely intended to prevent this. Owing to the enormous amount of ground to be covered, a major role in this operation was assigned to XIX Tactical Air Command, which conducted repeated sorties along the Loire to look for German activity. In addition, the US Army Air Force systematically destroyed bridges over the Loire to prevent any German flank attacks.

As a result of the actions of Patton's three corps, by August 24, the Seine had been breached both north and south of Paris. Instead of attempting to set up a comprehensive defensive line behind Paris, AOK 1 was ordered to conduct counterattacks against the bridgeheads over the next few days using weak and unprepared formations. This did little to halt the American advance, and led to the rapid attrition of the Wehrmacht units involved, speeding the rout of AOK 1 in the area northeast of Paris in the final week of August.

The situation of AOK 1 was all the more crucial as it was intended to be the link between Army Group B and the retreating elements of Army Group G from southern and central France. The rapid advance of the US Seventh Army out of its Operation *Dragoon* beachhead on the Riviera threatened to

The 11th Infantry Regiment, 5th Infantry Division, pushed into Fontainebleau on August 23 after having beaten off the main counterattack by the German 48.Infanterie Division the day before. Here, wary infantrymen advance behind the cover of an M10 3in. GMC of the 818th Tank Destroyer Battalion. (NARA)

The battle for Chartres: August 15–18, 1944

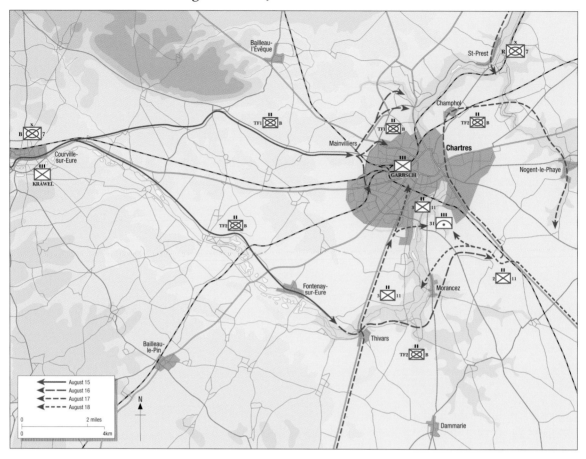

push up along the Swiss and German frontier, essentially cutting off all of the rest of the Wehrmacht in France including the First and Nineteenth Armies. On the morning of August 17, Berlin sent an urgent message to Army Group G authorizing a full-scale retreat west to the Seine River. It was amplified further the next morning, instructing all German forces in southern and central France to withdraw to the south wing of Army Group B, namely AOK 1's precarious defense line on the Seine, with the exception of fortress troops in fortified harbors such as Toulon and Marseilles along the Südwall, and Atlantic coast fortified ports such as Royan and Lorient. These orders essentially acknowledged that the Wehrmacht was abandoning about two-thirds of France without a fight.

A SIMMERING PARIS SUMMER

Tensions in Paris rose steadily through the summer as evidence of German troubles mounted. Parisians celebrated the national holiday of July 14 for the first time since the Occupation began with a gigantic, unorganized outpouring into the streets. Tricolor flags and badges blossomed, and to the dismay of the Germans, some of the French police joined in the celebrations. The communist FTP began to step up their sabotage actions around the city, aided by the most stubborn and belligerent of the trade unions, the railway workers. The Paris insurrection continued its slow boil on August 3 when the railmen

The US Army approaches Paris: August 19–24, 1944

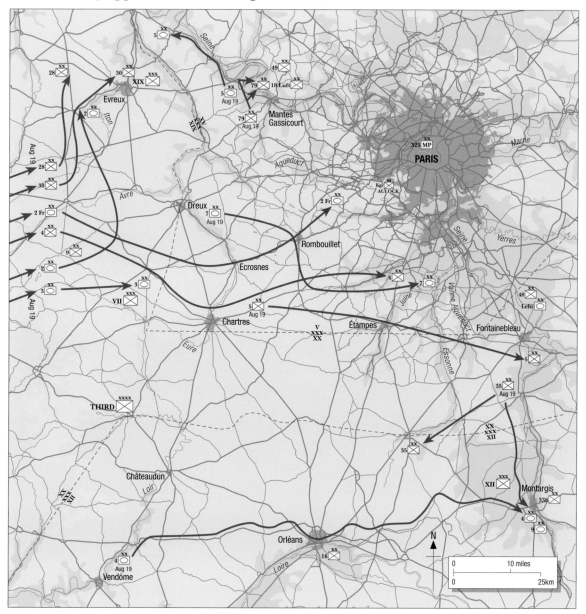

threatened a strike. They demanded that political prisoners be freed, that they be allotted a half-kilo of bread each day and that three months' wages be paid in advance. Recognizing that capitulation would simply lead to similar demands by other trade unions, the Germans refused. The rail strike began on August 10 at the 17 main rail depots, bringing transport in the city area to a halt. It was the first major strike in Paris since the Occupation began and neither the Germans nor the French Milice were able to break it by force.

By the second week of August 1944, it was obvious to the average Parisian that the Germans were abandoning the city. The "grey mice," the uniformed women of the Wehrmacht, had disappeared, as had most German civilian employees. German offices in the center of the city were burning their files in the courtyards. Day by day, more and more German headquarters

A .30in. light machine-gun team takes up positions behind hay stacks in a field "somewhere in France" on August 23. (NARA)

BELOW RIGHT
A German motorized column knocked out while attempting to attack the 11th Infantry Regiment on the approaches to Fontainebleau on August 23. In the foreground is a Volkswagen Kübelwagen while behind are a StuG III assault gun and a burned-out half-track with anti-aircraft gun. (NARA)

were evacuated eastward, leaving abandoned offices throughout the city. The unreliability of the French police was a growing concern to German commanders throughout northern France, and in early August, Kluge decided to conduct a surprise disarmament on Sunday, August 13. This action was the immediate catalyst for the Paris uprising.

The French learned about the plan shortly before it was carried out. It was impossible to conduct such an operation instantaneously throughout Paris because of the large size of the Parisian police force compared with the small number of troops available to the German army and police. The first disarmament actions in Paris took place on August 13 in the tough working-class neighborhoods of St. Denis, St. Ouen and Asnières first involving only about 375 policemen. By the end of the day, the Germans had collected about 5,000 revolvers. This prompted a meeting of the key Parisian resistance leadership including Col. Rol, de Gaulle's emissary Alexandre Parodi, and the leaders of the three main police resistance groups. The French leaders

LEFT
Under fire, engineers ferry a 1½-ton truck of the 10th Infantry Regiment over the Seine River near Montreau on August 25, with splashes from the gunfire evident in the water. (NARA)

BELOW LEFT
The first senior US commander over the Seine was George Patton seen here in his jeep crossing the treadway bridge near Melun on August 26. (NARA)

were all aware that the armed police were potentially a decisive element in any uprising since the French resistance had so few weapons in Paris. The FFI leadership called for a police strike, instructing the police to keep their weapons and join the resistance. The police were in a tricky position since the Germans had shown no compunction in shooting anyone associated with the resistance. It was equally clear that the Germans would soon be out of Paris and the FFI warned police who disobeyed their instructions that they would be considered collaborators.

The police strike took effect on August 14, and only a small number of police showed up for duty. That day, Choltitz took over command of Greater Paris from the disgraced Gen.Lt. von Boineburg. Hitler again instructed Choltitz that Paris was to be destroyed if necessary, but there were still no signs of any reinforcements for the feeble Paris garrison beyond instructions that a powerful Karl mortar would be moved to the city for potential action. Choltitz's first action was a parade of troops and Panzers on Monday

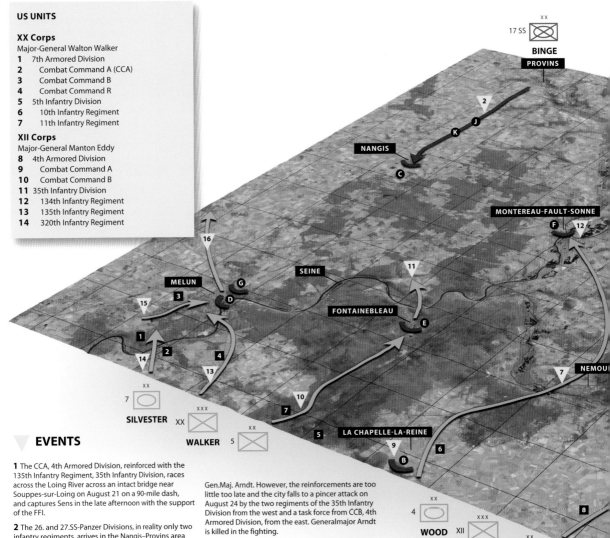

US UNITS

XX Corps
Major-General Walton Walker
1. 7th Armored Division
2. Combat Command A (CCA)
3. Combat Command B
4. Combat Command R
5. 5th Infantry Division
6. 10th Infantry Regiment
7. 11th Infantry Regiment

XII Corps
Major-General Manton Eddy
8. 4th Armored Division
9. Combat Command A
10. Combat Command B
11. 35th Infantry Division
12. 134th Infantry Regiment
13. 135th Infantry Regiment
14. 320th Infantry Regiment

▼ EVENTS

1 The CCA, 4th Armored Division, reinforced with the 135th Infantry Regiment, 35th Infantry Division, races across the Loing River across an intact bridge near Souppes-sur-Loing on August 21 on a 90-mile dash, and captures Sens in the late afternoon with the support of the FFI.

2 The 26. and 27.SS-Panzer Divisions, in reality only two infantry regiments, arrives in the Nangis–Provins area on August 22, and are used by AOK 1 to rejuvenate the skeletal 17.SS-Panzergrenadier Division.

3 A battalion from the newly arrived 17.SS-Panzergrenadier Division attempts to counterattack CCA, 4th Armored Division, in Sens on August 22, but is caught en route and routed with heavy casualties. CCA heads east towards Troyes, which falls on August 25.

4 A task force from CCB, 4th Armored Division, advances on Courtenay and takes the town on the afternoon of August 22.

5 The 35th Infantry Division begins an advance on Montargis from the west, with the 320th Infantry Regiment first taking Pithiviers before joining the 134th Infantry Regiment in the attack on Montargis.

6 A second task force from CCB, 4th Armored Division, approaches Montargis from the northeast, but is held up by German resistance in Paucourt which falls on August 23.

7 Local FFI units liberate Nemours on August 23.

8 The newly arrived Grenadier Regimenter 757 and 758 from the 338.Infanterie Division reinforce the Kampfgruppe of the 708.Infanterie Division under Gen.Maj. Arndt. However, the reinforcements are too little too late and the city falls to a pincer attack on August 24 by the two regiments of the 35th Infantry Division from the west and a task force from CCB, 4th Armored Division, from the east. Generalmajor Arndt is killed in the fighting.

9 The 10th Infantry Regiment, 5th Infantry Division, pushes through a battalion of the German Sicherungs Regiment 1010 at Malesherbes on August 21, resuming the attack towards La Chapelle-la-Reine on August 22.

10 On August 21, the 11th Infantry Regiment, 5th Infantry Division, encounters heavy opposition from a Flak battalion and elements of AOK 1 z.b.v and skirts the city. The next day, 11th Infantry Regiment is counterattacked by a Kampfgruppe from Fontainebleau leading to a day of fighting on the outskirts of the city.

11 The 11th Infantry Regiment pushes into Fontainebleau on August 23, and begins sending troops over the Seine by improvised means. An entire battalion is over the river by August 24, and engineers assemble a treadway bridge.

12 With resistance in Fontainebleau crumbling and Nemours liberated by the FFI, the 10th Infantry Regiment is sent to Montereau, which is cleared on August 24.

13 CCR, 7th Armored Division, arrives on outskirts of Melun on August 22, while CCA is held up by artillery fire further west near Arpajon. The last remaining bridge is blown up around 0800hrs on August 23, but later in the day the 38th Armored Infantry Battalion sends a company over to the island in the Seine and clears the southern sections of the town.

14 The CCA, 7th Armored Division, arrives near Tilly on August 23; the 48th Armored Infantry Battalion sends troops across in assault boats. Engineers begin building a treadway bridge that afternoon but it is not completed until 0900hrs on August 24 due to intense artillery bombardment. Once completed, CCB moves over the Seine to prepare for assault from the northeast.

15 CCR begins attacks into town on the morning of August 24 against modest opposition. CCB begins moving into Melun from the northwest at 0200hrs on August 25, but delayed by minefields, it enters the town around 0715hrs by morning. Last pockets of resistance are cleared by morning.

16 7th Armored Division begins a broad assault from Melun to exploit the bridgehead at 1900hrs August 25, aiming for Reims.

RACE FOR THE SEINE SOUTH OF PARIS: AUGUST 21–25, 1944
The US XX and XII corps at Melun and Montereau

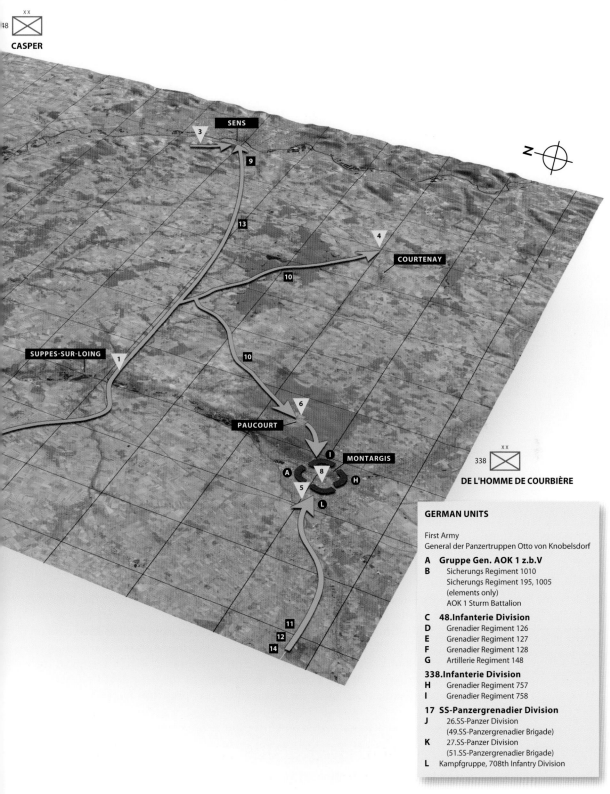

Note: Gridlines are shown at intervals of 3.10 miles/5km

CASPER

SENS

COURTENAY

SUPPES-SUR-LOING

PAUCOURT

MONTARGIS

DE L'HOMME DE COURBIÈRE

GERMAN UNITS

First Army
General der Panzertruppen Otto von Knobelsdorf

A   Gruppe Gen. AOK 1 z.b.V
B   Sicherungs Regiment 1010
      Sicherungs Regiment 195, 1005
      (elements only)
      AOK 1 Sturm Battalion

C   48.Infanterie Division
D   Grenadier Regiment 126
E   Grenadier Regiment 127
F   Grenadier Regiment 128
G   Artillerie Regiment 148

338.Infanterie Division
H   Grenadier Regiment 757
I   Grenadier Regiment 758

17 SS-Panzergrenadier Division
J   26.SS-Panzer Division
      (49.SS-Panzergrenadier Brigade)
K   27.SS-Panzer Division
      (51.SS-Panzergrenadier Brigade)
L   Kampfgruppe, 708th Infantry Division

53

German fortifications in Paris were quite modest, with roadblocks and other obstructions being a more common means of defense as seen here. (NARA)

afternoon around the Opéra in the center of Paris. Parisians greeted this menacing display with derision. Choltitz projected a brutal face to the French public, posting notices that acts of violence against German troops would be met with brutal force. But in reality, he did not have the resources to patrol the city regularly. German troops walked the streets of the city at risk of their own safety and most of the patrolling was done by car or armored vehicle. Choltitz hoped to keep the city calm by a "live and let live" policy. He called in Paris city officials on August 16 and asked for their cooperation in maintaining peace and order. It was vital for the city services—water, electricity, gas and food—to continue as much for the sake of the Parisians as the dwindling number of German troops. In return, he promised the French officials that "Paris would be neither defended nor destroyed, nor delivered to looting and arson." As strike fever spread, the postal workers went out on August 16, and the Metro workers on August 17. The final mass evacuation of German personnel took place on August 17, followed the next day by the last senior German police and Nazi functionaries including SS police chief Oberg. The lack of subway and bus services as well as trade union actions brought most of the industries in Paris to a halt by August 18. The last meeting of the ministers of the Vichy French government under Pierre Laval took place on August 17, and that day, German authorities "invited" the doddering old Maréchal Pétain to depart for Alsace. There were few illusions on either side about what was about to transpire.

While Choltitz and the French municipal leadership tried to keep a lid on a likely revolt, diplomatic efforts were underway to declare Paris an open city as had been the case in 1940. The Paris mayor, Pierre Tattinger, had already been trying to convince the consuls of the neutral states, notably Spain, Switzerland and Sweden, to apply pressure on their German colleagues. The Swedish consul, Raoul Nordling, was especially active in this regard. The decision rested on Hitler, but he was in such a foul temper since the bomb plot that conciliation was inconceivable. Nordling also attempted to deal with the possibility that French political prisoners might be massacred and began feverish attempts to win their freedom.

On August 16, the principal leaders of the communist PCF met and decided to call for a full-scale insurrection on Saturday, August 19. The PCF decided to force the hand of the other resistance groups, even though de Gaulle's government in London had already issued orders against an uprising until the Allies were at the gates of the city. Warsaw had staged an insurrection starting on August 1, and the Germans had responded in brutal fashion with tens of thousands of civilian dead by the middle of the month. De Gaulle's government feared that a premature call for insurrection would lead to a similar tragedy. Although committed to a revolt as soon as possible, the PCF did not control the Paris police, so they agreed to a meeting with other resistance leaders on Friday, August 18. The communist leader André Tollet pushed for insurrection but was initially opposed by Gaullist leaders such as Alexandre Parodi. But the Gaullists quickly realized that a revolt was going to happen with or without their approval, either an uncontrolled spontaneous revolt in scattered areas of the city or a unified event that they might be able to influence. By the end of the meeting, Parodi and the Gaullists agreed with the communists' plan to call for action on Saturday, August 19.

THE REVOLT BEGINS

Even though the communists had initiated the revolt, it was quickly out of their hands. The Gaullists realized that the police formed the largest single armed French group in the city and were determined that the new government would control them. The key event in the revolt would be the seizure of the Prefecture of Police located in the heart of the city on the Île de la Cité near Notre Dame cathedral. About 2,000 policemen congregated to take over the prefecture at 0700hrs the next morning from the Vichy prefect, Amédée Bussière. Colonel Rol turned up at the prefecture without any knowledge of the planned takeover, and at first was turned away. Rol turned his attention to the insurrection gradually unfolding elsewhere in the city. In reality, the FFI teams were modest in numbers and firepower, and limited in their ability to conduct attacks on the German garrisons. Instead, the FFI plan was to seize the town halls (*mairies*) in Paris's 20 main districts (*arrondissements*). Gunfire broke out all through Paris on August 19, and there were numerous small-scale clashes between the FFI and German troops. The French were especially keen to ambush trucks and depots where they might obtain small arms.

In the afternoon, a German counterattack began to take shape as a group from Sicherungs Regiment 5 attempted to retake the police prefecture, supported by tanks from Panzer Kompanie Paris. However, the German detachment did not have enough infantry to rush the building and a stalemate ensued. When this attack failed, Choltitz decided to launch a full-scale assault on the prefecture preceded by a Luftwaffe attack. By the time the decision was made, it was already evening, so the assault was put off until Sunday morning. Another major skirmish occurred at the Neuilly town hall, which was first captured by the FFI, but then recaptured when Oberst Jay sent a detachment of 150 troops and tanks to the site. The day's fighting was largely a draw. The FFI had neither the arms nor organization to take control of the city, nor did the Germans have the resources to pry the FFI out of the municipal buildings they had seized. The police force in the prefecture was almost out of ammunition by the end of the day with little prospect of acquiring any more. The last major municipal building, the Hôtel de Ville,

ATTACK ON THE POLICE PREFECTURE: AUGUST 19, 1944 (pp. 56–57)

Following the seizure of the police prefecture on the Île de la Cité in the morning, Choltitz ordered the building recaptured. Sicherungs Regiment 5 had its hands full with the city erupting into fighting, but managed to put together a small task force of infantry supported by three tanks, which launched their attack around 1530hrs in the afternoon. Reports on the type of tanks vary, but the attack may have included one Panther. In the event, the main combatants were a pair of PzKpfw 35Rs, the German designation for the Renault R-35 infantry tanks captured in 1940 (1). These were easier to move around the city than the dozen Panthers on hand, especially over the Seine bridges and in narrower streets in the older parts of the city. While its 37mm gun was obsolete for the 1944 battlefield, it was more than adequate when fighting against poorly armed insurgents. Curiously enough, French accounts suggest that the German tanks only fired armor-piercing ammunition, not the best solution against troops in buildings where high-explosive rounds are the preferred choice. It is unclear if this was Choltitz' policy or simply a lack of the proper ammunition. The scene here shows the tanks advancing along the side of the prefecture on Marché Neuf, the narrow street between the prefecture and the Seine River, with the accompanying infantry trying to engage the policemen holed up in the building.

In the event, the 2,000 policemen holed up in the massive structure were very poorly armed, equipped with only service revolvers, a small number of rifles and a few Hotchkiss machine guns (2). The only anti-tank weapons on hand were Molotov cocktails. By this point in time, the Molotov cocktail had progressed from being a simple bottle of gasoline with a flaming rag to ignite it, to a safer contraption using liquid acid mixed with the gasoline and a small packet of dry chemical on the outside which ignited the gasoline when the bottle was smashed. The famous scientist and political activist Frédéric Joliot-Curie, son-in-law of the legendary Madame Curie, undertook the manufacture of these refined Molotov cocktails. Although available to the police in large number, the Molotov cocktails were not especially dangerous as they were only effective as far as they could be thrown. Even then, their lethality against tanks depended upon whether they struck a portion of the tank where their fiery contents could seep inside. The police managed to disable at least one of the tanks with a Molotov cocktail (3), persuading the remaining tanks to keep their distance.

By early evening, the battle was a stand-off. On the one hand, the police in the prefecture were nearly out of ammunition except for Molotov cocktails. On the other hand, the prefecture was a solidly built structure, designed to resist mob violence and so proof against all but a determined infantry attack. The Sicherungs Regiment 5 troops (4) were mostly older men with little enthusiasm to die for the Führer, and by nightfall, they withdrew to await further orders and reinforcements.

The seizure of the police prefecture on the Île de la Cité made this the center of the initial fighting. Here, FFI troops take up positions behind a modest barricade on the Pont Neuf leading to the island, with the Eiffel Tower evident in the background. (NARA)

was seized by the FFI in the early hours of Sunday, August 20, and it was assigned to the leadership of the CNR.

Parodi and the Gaullists were already convinced that the uprising was premature and wanted to buy time. After meeting early on Sunday morning and agreeing to propose a truce and they called together as many CNR members as they could reach and held an impromptu meeting; none of the more militant communists were present. They contacted the Swedish consul, Raoul Nordling, who had Choltitz' ear. On Sunday morning, Nordling visited Choltitz at his headquarters at the Hotel Meurice and proposed a truce "to pick up the dead and wounded." Although Choltitz was not immediately in favor of the idea, Nordling was able to convince him of its merits. Choltitz did not have enough troops to maintain order in Paris, and even an attack on the prefecture would strain his resources. A truce would leave him in control of most of the city, even if the insurgents had footholds in a few dozen buildings scattered across the city. The agreement had four main points: the FFI would be recognized as regular troops subject to the Geneva convention; the Germans would not contest FFI control of municipal buildings so long as the truce was in force; likewise the FFI would not attack German strongpoints; finally, and most importantly for Choltitz, the FFI would not interfere with German convoys moving through Paris. The CNR agreed to the truce at 1030hrs, but there was little support from the armed FFI leaders. In the afternoon, the Seine department FFI commander, Colonel Lizé, declared such discussions with Choltitz as "treason" and the COMAC FFI military command voted against accepting the truce later in the evening. Curiously enough, Parodi and two other French representatives were arrested by a German patrol on Sunday afternoon while accompanying a loudspeaker truck announcing the truce, and dragged before Choltitz. Nordling was present at the meeting and explained to the German commander who they were, arguing that they must be released. Choltitz finally agreed, and Parodi and his companions were freed that evening.

By Monday, August 21, the truce was only partly in effect. Numerous skirmishes occurred around Paris instigated by FFI groups who did not accept the ceasefire and by scattered German detachments out of touch with headquarters. The FFI seized several more buildings including the Élysée Palace and the Gare de l'Est railroad station. Still short of arms, the FFI had requested a US airdrop to assist the insurrection. The USAAF planned to conduct Operation *Beggar* on Tuesday, August 22, by the "Carpetbaggers"— the 492nd Bombardment Group specially trained in arms drops. The plan was to use 130 B-24 bombers to deliver about 200 tons of arms into Paris around the Bois de Boulogne, Auteuil, Longchamp, the park in front of the

Paris uprising: August 19–24, 1944

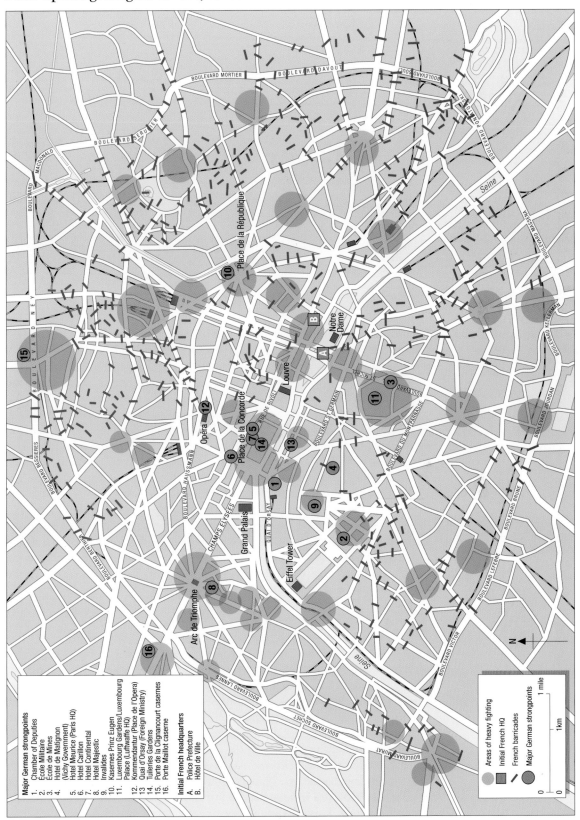

Major German strongpoints
1. Chamber of Deputies
2. Ecole Militaire
3. Ecole de Mines
4. Hôtel de Matignon (Vichy Government)
5. Hôtel Meurice (Paris HQ)
6. Hôtel Carillon
7. Hôtel Continental
8. Hôtel Majestic
9. Invalides
10. Kasernes Prinz Eugen
11. Luxembourg Gardens/Luxembourg Palace (Luftwaffe HQ)
12. Kommendantur (Place de l'Opera)
13. Quai d'Orsay (Foreign Ministry)
14. Tuileries Gardens
15. Porte de la Clignancourt casernes
16. Porte Maillot caserne

Initial French headquarters
A. Police Prefecture
B. Hôtel de Ville

Legend:
Areas of heavy fighting
Initial French HQ
French barricades
Major German strongpoints

0 1km
0 1 mile

An FFI patrol, including armed policeman, take up positions against nearby German snipers. (NARA)

Invalides and other locations. This airdrop was postponed a day by Général Koenig who feared that it would provoke a major German counterattack when the FFI tried to recover the parachutes, and there was also concern that many of the arms would actually fall into German hands. In the end, the airdrops were never conducted.

The Wehrmacht response to the uprising was feeble because of the lack of resources following the calamitous Falaise encirclement. On August 19, Gerneralfeldmarschall Model of OB West allotted a paltry two battalions of the 6.Fallschirmjäger Division to Paris along with two mobile artillery units. The 9.Panzer Division was instructed to conduct its rebuilding effort in the Paris area. Three units from the Fifteenth Army on the Pas de Calais were assigned to the defense of the Seine River line on either side of Paris, the 47., 48. and 49.Infanterie Divisionen. That evening, Model bluntly informed Berlin that Paris could not be held with existing forces in the face of a major insurrection. Neither Model nor Berlin had a clear appreciation of the events in Paris and were unaware of the depth of US Army penetrations toward the Seine on either side of the city.

A CHANGE OF PLANS

Even if the uprising had spread throughout the city, the FFI was incapable of attacking the main German strongholds. On the other hand, Choltitz's bedraggled units had little hope of pushing the FFI out of their strongholds either. The Gaullists such as Parodi hoped for a quick entry for the US Army, while Col. Rol and the communists still hoped that the city might be liberated before the Americans arrived. The main Gaullist leaders were in contact with de Gaulle via radio during the insurrection, and a number of groups independently sent out delegations in hope of reaching the American lines to convince them to intervene quickly. One of the most important of these was the effort by Col. Rol to send his chief of staff Commandant Gallois-Cocteau to reach Patton's Third Army in hope of convincing the US Army to conduct

an airdrop of weapons to the FFI on the plaza in front of Notre Dame cathedral. Gallois succeeded in reaching Patton's headquarters in the early hours of Tuesday, August 22, but Patton reiterated the official US plan: the city would be bypassed and the US Army was primarily concerned with routing the Wehrmacht and reluctant to take on the responsibility of feeding the city when its own forward troops were still short of supplies and fuel. Impressed by the intensity of the young French officer, Patton sent him to Gen. Bradley's headquarters where he arrived around 0900hrs. He was questioned by Bradley's intelligence chief, Brigadier-General Edwin Sibert, who revealed that Bradley and Eisenhower were about to hold a meeting to discuss this very issue. Gallois's eloquent plea was one of many from French military leaders, including a personal plea from de Gaulle to Eisenhower during a meeting on August 20 when he informed Ike that he had already "ordered" the 2e DB to advance on Paris. The most curious entreaty to Eisenhower, but one that in the end had no influence in the decision, was from Choltitz himself. On the morning of Tuesday, August 22, Choltitz summoned Raoul Nordling and hinted that he should travel to the American side to urge the US Army to proceed to Paris as quickly as possible. He revealed that he had received more orders from Hitler to destroy the city and would have to do so in a day or two or be relieved of command. Choltitz was playing a double game: informing Berlin of his plans to dynamite the city in the event that reinforcements did arrive, but limiting his actions to demolish the city in the more likely case that the Allies arrived first. Although he could not put anything in writing, he informed Nordling that "what I am really doing is asking the Allies to help me." Overwhelmed by the frantic activity of the past few days, Nordling suffered a mild heart attack that prevented him from going but he dispatched his brother in his place, using a German driver. However, they arrived after Eisenhower had already made his decision.

During the meeting on August 22, Bradley and Eisenhower agreed that the situation in Paris was getting out of hand and that they would have to intervene regardless of previous planning. Eisenhower had already promised

During his meeting on August 20, de Gaulle pressed Eisenhower to include Paris in the immediate plans for Allied operations along the Seine. (NARA)

that Leclerc's 2e DB would be given the honor, but Bradley wanted it reinforced given Leclerc's penchant for independent action. The meeting also discussed tactical issues such as the awkward extension of Patton's Third Army into the British 21st Army Group sector at the Mantes bridgehead. So to permit Patton to continue his spectacular advance eastward, Bradley transferred Haislip's XV Corps to Hodges' First Army, and assigned the Paris mission to Gerow's V Corps as part of First Army. To accompany Leclerc's 2e DB, Bradley transferred "Tubby" Barton's reliable and experienced 4th Infantry Division from VII Corps to V Corps. The orders stated that the city was to be entered only if enemy resistance was such that it could be overcome with a light force. To avoid destruction of the city, there would be no severe fighting, and no air or artillery bombardment. Indeed, Gerow ordered the reduction of artillery battalions from the force to discourage excessive artillery use. The march orders were issued shortly before midnight on Tuesday evening.

The orders called for the 60-mile advance to be conducted in two columns. The North Column departing from Sees toward St. Cyr would consist of Leclerc's 2e DB minus one of its *groupements tactiques*, spearheaded by a troop from the 102nd Cavalry Squadron, supported by the 1121st Engineer Combat Group with its three battalions to help with road clearing and bridging, and the 190th Field Artillery Group with four artillery battalions. The South Column departing from Alençon toward Villacoublay would consist of the remaining *groupement tactique* from the 2e DB led by the rest of the 102nd Cavalry Group, and the 4th Infantry Division reinforced with the 70th Tank Battalion, 801st and 893rd Tank Destroyer Battalions, plus two anti-aircraft battalions.

Leclerc had already dispatched a small reconnaissance detachment under Lieutenant-Colonel Jacques de Guillebon toward Paris on August 21, consisting of a squadron with 10 light tanks, 10 armored cars, and an infantry section with 150 troops on half-tracks. The V Corps commander, Leonard Gerow, was infuriated when he learned about this and ordered Leclerc to withdraw this force, an order which Leclerc ignored. This incident would lead to strained relations between Gerow and Leclerc over the course of the next few days' operations. Guillebon's task force reached as far as Rambouillet where it waited for Leclerc's arrival on August 23.

TO THE BARRICADES!

By Monday, August 21, the ceasefire had collapsed and fighting resumed through much of the city. In the evening, Col. Lizé ordered the FFI to begin erecting barricades through the city, a tactic inspired by the Spanish Civil War battles in Barcelona. The Wehrmacht units had been using Panzer Kompanie Paris as well as armed trucks as a mobile force to attack various FFI strongpoints, and the barricades were intended to limit the movement of

German reinforcements. These were created using cobblestones, debris, burned automobiles and anything else on hand. In total some 400 major barricades were erected.

Choltitz received more threatening messages from Berlin instructing him to defend Paris to the last man and to prepare to destroy all the Seine River bridges and to reduce Paris to ruins. With the Allies already encircling Paris, and the outcome preordained, Choltitz had made up his mind to ignore Hitler's apocalyptic demands. Yet he was in a predicament as his family was still in Germany and might be subject to recriminations if he was deemed insufficiently obedient to Hitler's orders. He expected that the main phone lines to and from Army Group B headquarters in Margival were being monitored by the Gestapo since the July 20 bomb plot, so he called his colleague Hans Speidel and related how he was planning to blow up the Arc de Triomphe, the Opéra, the Eiffel Tower and other monuments. They had discussed Hitler's deranged mental state a few weeks before, and the phone conversation was a ruse. Choltitz had more assets for demolition than he admitted, but less than what was needed for a truly comprehensive scheme of destruction. The Kriegsmarine had a large torpedo depot near Paris in St. Cloud to support the navy bases on the French coast, and these included enough large warheads to do some serious damage. Boineberg had earlier refused to deploy these weapons, and at this late date, Choltitz did not have enough trained engineers to fuze or plant them, nor did he have the freedom to dispatch demolition teams around the city. Attempts to mine the Chamber of Deputies using the torpedo warheads was frustrated by FFI ambushes, which stopped every single truck sent out on August 24.

The fighting on Tuesday, August 22, was the fiercest since the start of the uprising, though not especially well organized by either side. A few tanks from Panzer Kompanie Paris attacked the Hôtel de Ville where the CNR had set up an alternative headquarters to Parodi's Gaullist HQ at the police prefecture. Lacking a determined infantry force, the German tanks fired a number of rounds and trundled off.

Although French radio in London announced the liberation of Paris by the FFI around noontime, this was wishful thinking. One of the largest German attacks was staged on Wednesday, August 23, against the Grand Palais, and

One of the lessons of the Spanish Civil War, and previous Paris insurrections, was the value of street barricades to limit the mobility of an occupying army. These were made from paving stones and whatever else was available. (NARA)

tank fire ignited a major conflagration. The Wehrmacht used Goliath remote-control demolition vehicles in the attack. In the midst of the fighting, French firefighters attempted to quell the blaze, and the fighting died down shortly before noon when the FFI abandoned the blazing structure. The most intense fighting that afternoon centered on the main post office, which successfully resisted a desultory bombardment by German tanks. The FFI launched one of its few major attacks on a German stronghold when units assaulted the Kaserne Prinz Eugen located on the Place de la République but the attack was beaten off with tank support. A Luftwaffe plan to bomb various FFI strongholds was continually put off as Luftflotte 3 insisted on conducting the attacks at night for fear of Allied fighters, and Choltitz insisted they attack during the day when they might actually have a chance of hitting something.

A typical Paris resistance group, consisting of FFI members as well as police, parading on the Place de la Concorde on August 25. (NARA)

In exasperation, Choltitz threatened to withdraw the army troops from the areas to be bombed and place the blame on the Luftwaffe for the retreat. As a result, no bombing raids occurred. In the late afternoon, a light artillery spotter aircraft of the 2e DB flew over the embattled police prefecture and dropped a note from Leclerc saying simply "Tenez bon. Nous arrivons"— "Hold on. We're coming."

Hitler's instructions to Choltitz on August 23 were blunt:

> The defense of Paris and its bridgehead was of decisive military and political importance. Their loss would tear open the whole coastal front and deprive Germany of the base for V-weapons. History showed that the loss of Paris meant the loss of all France. The sharpest measures must be taken against the first signs of insurrection—public execution of the ringleaders. ... Demolition of the Seine bridges must be prepared. Paris must never fall into Allied hands or only as a heap of rubble.

THE ADVANCE OF THE 2e DIVISION BLINDÉE

The main staging area for the advance of the 2e DB was around Rambouillet, located about 22 miles from the southwest edge of Paris. Given the size of the division, it took most of August 23 to move it from its original positions around Sées to the staging area, some units moving as much as 125 miles. Leclerc planned to advance on the city in two columns, GTL led by Colonel Langlade heading toward Porte St. Cloud on the southwest periphery of Paris, and GTV led by Colonel Bilotte aiming for Porte d'Orléans on the southern edge with both columns to converge on Place de la Concorde in the heart of the city. This did not conform exactly to Gerow's instructions, but was based on a better appreciation of the geography of Paris. The center of gravity for any attack on Paris was the cluster of government facilities on the Île de la Cité, the neighboring Quai d'Orsay, and the Palais du Luxembourg. The Gerow plan had the attack focused too far west toward the largely residential and industrial neighborhoods, perhaps based on the mistaken idea that the Eiffel Tower is the center of Paris. Leclerc modified the details of Gerow's orders, but kept their intent of facilitating a rapid liberation of Paris. Unfortunately, he never conveyed these changes to Gerow who suspected subversion and incompetence in Leclerc's modifications.

Both 2e DB columns began their advance on the morning of Wednesday, August 24, around 0630hrs, with rain falling through most of the area. The advance guard of Lt. Col. Guillebon had already scouted the roads toward Versailles and had found the road north out of Rambouillet to be blocked a few miles out of the city by German defenses while the route through the Chevreuse Valley appeared to be more accessible. Although V Corps' orders had specified the route via St. Cyr to the north, Leclerc decided to send Langlade's GTL up the less protected Route 189. A small diversionary force under Commandant François Morel-Deville was sent up the road toward St. Cyr to "make noise." Bilotte's GTV started from positions farther east near Arpajon and headed up Route 20 into the south of Paris.

Although the German forces in the area were not crack troops, the approach route was heavily urbanized, forcing motorized units to stick to the roads. Boineberg had anticipated this in his defense plans, and most of the main roads were covered by Flak batteries protected by small detachments of troops from Kampfgruppe Aulock. These included both 88mm guns and numerous 20mm automatic cannon. The French tankers found the Flak batteries and occasional tanks to be formidable opponents, the half-hearted security battalions less so. Bilotte's GTV was led by an advance guard to seize the bridge at Longjumeau. The town was taken by 1000hrs with about 250 prisoners. At this point, Bilotte's GTV was split into two task forces under Colonels Putz and Warabiot in order to take advantage of the numerous smaller roads leading into the city. Shortly after exiting Longjumeau, Putz's columns came under intense anti-tank fire from about a dozen 88mm Flak guns stations in the vicinity of Massy and Wissous on the edge of the Orly airfield. These had to be reduced methodically with scarce infantry and about 500 prisoners were taken.

The 2e DB encountered the strongest German resistance along the southern route into the city on August 23. This M8 light armored car is seen overlooking a German street barricade in Antony in the Paris suburbs. (NARA)

The advance on Paris: August 23–24, 1944

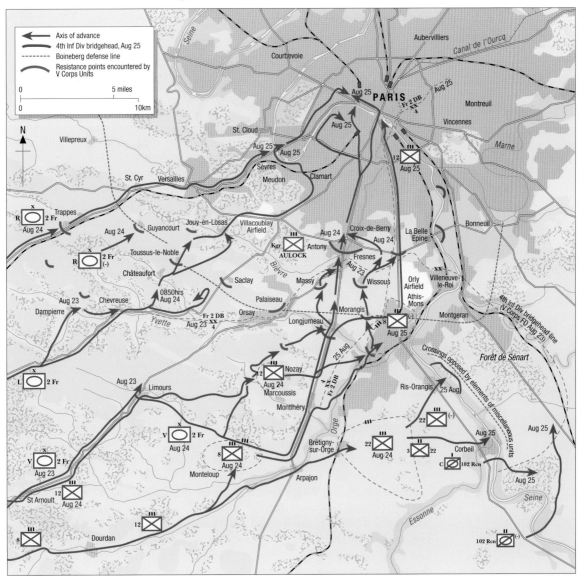

   In the meantime, Warabiot's *détachement* headed out from the east of Longjumeau via Savigny-sur-Orge. His troops reduced the German defenses around Wissous, which also helped to free up the route of advance of Putz's columns to the west. Kampfgruppe Aulock attempted to counterattack, sending a truck-mounted infantry column down the road from Choisy-le-Roi but it was caught in the open by French tanks and destroyed. The most stubbornly defended strongpoint encountered that afternoon was in Fresnes, based around a solidly built prison. It was a key part of a heavily defended zone straddling Route 20, which included the nearby town of Antony and the crossroads at Croix-de-Berny. By the end of the day, Bilotte's GTV had overcome most of the defenses at the Croix-de-Berny crossroads where it would spend the night. Bilotte decided against any further actions that evening as most of his men had been on the move for 48 hours and needed some rest before the anticipated fighting in the city the next day.

A column of M4A2 tanks of Bilotte's GTV move down a street in Antony about six miles (10km) south of Paris on the afternoon of August 24, 1944. (NARA)

While Bilotte's GTV was moving on Paris from the south, Langlade's GTL was attempting to enter the city from the southwest. Its progress out of Rambouillet was rapid at first, moving quickly through Toussus-le-Noble but the columns quickly ran into the Flak belt of the Boineberg Line, held mainly by Fallschirmjäger Flak Regiment 11, which was headquartered nearby at Villacoublay airbase. As in the case of GTV, GTL divided into two task forces headed by Massu and Minjeonnet. By the end of the day, the columns fought their way to the Sèvres Bridge on the Seine and the area near the Renault factory on the edge of Paris by nightfall. As in the case of Bilotte's columns, Langlade ordered the unit to get some rest before the next day's climactic actions.

It had been Gerow's expectation that the 2e DB would enter Paris on August 24, and he lacked a clear picture of the progress of Leclerc's columns. Bradley had also expected that the city would be entered on Thursday, and pressed Gerow to get his troops moving. Although the 4th Infantry Division had been moved by truck toward Paris the day before, they were behind Billotte's troops and not expected to enter the city until after the 2e DB. In frustration with what he thought was Leclerc's slow progress, he ordered the 4th Infantry Division to move into the city as promptly as possible.

Leclerc was exasperated by the delays caused by the German defenses throughout Thursday, and insistent that at least some elements of the division reach the city center that day. In the early evening around 1930hrs, he turned to one of his most trusted soldiers, Capitaine Raymond Dronne, and instructed him to lead a small detachment into the city by way of the Porte d'Italie by avoiding the German defensive positions. Dronne's *détachement* consisted of three tanks, six half-tracks with elements of two infantry platoons and some miscellaneous engineer vehicles. Curiously it was the Spanish troops of the "Neuve," the 9e Compagnie of the RMT, who were given the honor of being the first into Paris. These were Republican veterans of the Spanish Civil War and amongst the most determined troops of the 2e DB. With the help of FFI members, the column stealthily made its way up Avenue d'Italie, across the Austerlitz Bridge and to the Hôtel de Ville where the CNR headquarters was

ABOVE
Infantry of the RMT engage German troops during fighting around Châteaufort in the southwest suburbs of Paris on August 24. (NARA)

LEFT
Général Leclerc with his characteristic walking stick watches as a column of M4A2 tanks of the 501e RCC pass by on August 24; beside him is his aide-de-camp, Capitaine Girard. (NARA)

Sitting on the Place de la Concorde was this lone Panther tank, which was first hit by a well-placed shot from an M10 tank destroyer near the Arc de Triomphe over a mile away. Moments later it was attacked and rammed by an M4A2 tank of the Branet *détachement*. (MHI)

located, finally arriving around 2120hrs as night was falling. The column sent some of its members to the police prefecture, and, on learning the news, the massive bells at Notre-Dame began to chime to announce their arrival, soon repeated by all the church bells in central Paris.

Choltitz called Speidel at OB West headquarters and held the telephone up to the sound of ringing bells. "The Allies have arrived." Choltitz asked Speidel to look after his family, anticipating the end was near. It was a disturbed night around Paris as the Flak batteries around the city fired incessantly; no major air raids were underway and there was some suspicion that the Paris garrison was simply firing off their ammunition before the inevitable capitulation. Choltitz ordered Aulock's *Kampfgruppe* on the Paris outskirts to withdraw behind the Seine. For the most part, these units ended up on the western side of Paris, mainly in the Versailles area. The end was approaching.

LIBERATING PARIS

Leclerc issued orders for the advance into Paris in the early hours of Friday, August 24. FFI members had infiltrated out of Paris over the past few days with very precise details of the disposition of German troops in Paris, right down to the location of individual tanks. The assignments for day were for Langlade's GTL to head northeast and seize the Étoile area at the head of the Champs Élysées, then converge down toward Place de la Concorde. Bilotte's GTV was given the principal assignment of moving to Île de la Cité, then advancing on the Hotel Meurice, Choltitz' headquarters on the Rue de Rivoli. Dio's GTD was assigned to follow behind GTV and attack the concentration of German troops around the École Militaire and the Invalides. Each of these combat commands were divided into task forces (*sous-groupements*) and further into *détachements* with specific assignments.

In contrast to the fighting on Thursday, the 2e DB columns met little resistance on Friday morning. Groupement Tactique V moved out of the Croix-de-Berny crossroads around 0715hrs, entered the city at Porte Gentilly, and reached the police prefecture at 0830hrs. If there was any delay, it was because of the ecstatic welcome from the Parisians. Groupement Tactique L had a somewhat longer drive from Pont de Sèvres, but reached the Étoile with little resistance. The US 4th Infantry Division likewise encountered only sporadic sniper fire, moving on the Gare d'Austerlitz in the city's eastern districts before heading for Place de la Bastille, and sending a reconnaissance group over toward Notre Dame to meet up with the 2e DB. Although the main body of the 2e DB was well within Paris by mid-morning, there was little evidence that the main strongholds in the center of the city would surrender without a fight. Probes toward these garrisons such as the École Militaire, the École des Mines, the Senate, the Kaserne Prinz Eugen and the Palais Bourbon were met with heavy small arms fire. Around 1000hrs, the three *groupements tactiques* consulted by radio and set out assignments for the afternoon's final advance into the heart of the city. A surrender note was sent to Choltitz who turned it down as premature.

The final assault began around 1300hrs. The centerpiece of the action was a push by a *détachement* of GTV led by Commandant Jean de la Horie down one of Paris' poshest streets, the Rue de Rivoli, which runs past the Louvre museum and the Tuileries gardens. Its principal assignment was to secure the surrender of Choltitz in the Hotel Meurice. A column of M4A2 tanks of the 3e Comapgnie, 501e RCC, under Capitaine Branet advanced down the Rue de Rivoli while an infantry *détachement* from the 3e Compagnie, 1/RMT, under Lieutenant Henri Karcher advanced under the cover of the famous arcades on the north side of the street. While tank fighting ensued on the street, and in the neighboring Tuileries garden, Karcher's infantrymen entered the Hotel Meurice. After a token exchange of gunfire and hand grenades, the German troops began to surrender. Karcher raced up the stairs to find Choltitz and the other senior officers of his command. In his excitement, Karcher blurted out "Do you speak German?" to which Choltitz responded "Of course I speak German!" In seconds, Karcher was followed by Commandant Jean de la Horie who asked Choltitz if he was prepared to surrender. The German officers had

An M4A2 tank from Bilotte's *groupement tactique* advances along the tree-lined banks of the Seine through an improvised barricade on August 24. (NARA)

RIGHT

The tanks of Panzer Kompanie Paris were amongst the most feared weapons available to the German defenders since the FFI had few weapons effective against them except for Molotov cocktails. The capture of these tanks was a major prize, and this shows one of the company's Renault R-40 tanks taken in the final days of the fighting. (NARA)

RIGHT

The tanks of Panzer Kompanie Paris were amongst the most feared weapons available to the German defenders since the FFI had few weapons effective against them except for Molotov cocktails. The capture of these tanks was a major prize, and this shows one of the company's Renault R-40 tanks taken in the final days of the fighting. (NARA)

BELOW RIGHT

An M4A2 tank named "Franche-Comté" of the 3/12e RCA receives an enthusiastic welcome as it advances down Avenue Victor Hugo on August 25. (NARA)

already laid out their weapons on the table, and Choltitz replied that he would surrender. Horie escorted Choltitz and the other senior staff officers out of the hotel, and had a hard time fighting through the angry French crowd to get them safely to the waiting jeep. They met Gén. Leclerc at the police prefecture with Col. Rol present for the formal surrender. Under the agreement, Choltitz agreed to surrender the whole Paris garrison and to send his emissaries out to the scattered strongpoints to inform them of the capitulation.

Choltitz's motivation during the Paris uprising have long been the subject of controversy. He was clearly disheartened by his meeting with Hitler in early August that revealed the depth of the Führer's growing mental imbalance. Distrustful of instructions from Berlin, he turned to his own

understanding of traditional rules of war to guide his actions in Paris. He was aware that the Wehrmacht had given up Rome without a fight in June 1944. In his later interrogation by US officers in Paris, he stated that he had "saved Paris for the Allies" and that he had put up only sufficient fight to convince his government that the city had not capitulated without honor. Choltitz clearly believed that Hitler's barbaric orders for the destruction of the city were a war crime. Some months later, British intelligence bugged a room where senior German officers were held, and overheard a conversation where Choltitz accused General der Fallschirmtruppe Hermann Ramke of war crimes for his actions leading to the destruction of Brest. In his memoirs, Choltitz discussed his unease with the senseless devastation of Paris, and

TANK ADVANCE ON THE RUE DE RIVOLI: AUGUST 24, 1944 (pp. 76–77)

The final attack to capture Choltitz' headquarters at the Hotel Meurice (1) began around 1300hrs on August 24. The attack was conducted by a *détachement* of the GTV led by Commandant Jean de la Horie down one of Paris' poshest streets, the Rue de Rivoli, which runs past the Louvre museum and the Tuileries gardens. The area was well defended with a pair of Panther tanks in the gardens, one on the Place de la Concorde, and a Renault R-35 tank (2) blocking the west end of the street where it opened to the Place de la Concorde. As a result, GTV deployed two tank columns, one down the street, and a second in parallel along the Seine embankment. The lead tank on the Rue de Rivoli was number 40, named "Douaumont" (3) from the 3e Compagnie, 501e RCC, commanded by Sergent Marcel Bizien (4). In an unequal struggle, the little Renault from Panzer Kompanie Paris was smashed with a single 75mm round which penetrated its rear, setting the engine compartment on fire. This is shown in the scene here. In the meantime, an infantry detachment from the 3e Compagnie, 1/RMT, under Lieutenant Henri Karcher advanced under the cover of the arcades on the north side of the street (5). The combat was not entirely one sided. A German soldier lobbed a grenade from the roof of one of the buildings, which bounced into the hatch of one of the five French Shermans, setting it on fire and seriously injuring the crew.

As the French tanks passed the Hotel Meurice and exited the Rue de Rivoli toward the Place de la Concorde, one of the most curious engagements of the battle for Paris took place. A single German Panther tank sat in the middle of the famous plaza, controlling the numerous streets and bridges that passed through it. While the Panther crew awaited the arrival of the French tanks from the Rue de Rivoli to the east, they did not notice that elements of GTL had taken up positions near the Arc de la Triomphe in the opposite direction. The crew of an M10 tank destroyer named "Simoun" spotted the Panther some 2,000 yards away and with remarkable precision or luck, managed to hit it on the tracks, damaging it and distracting the crew. At the same moment, "Douaumont" entered the plaza and charged the Panther, which was swiveling its turret towards them. "Douaumont" fired first, but its high-explosive round simply detonated on the Panther turret. In haste, "Douaumont's" gunner loaded a smoke shell instead of armor piercing, which enveloped the Panther in acrid white phosphorus smoke. In frustration, "Douaumont's" commander, Sergent Marcel Bizien, ordered the driver to ram the Panther. The two tanks were enveloped in the white smoke from the earlier projectile. Bizien leaped out of his turret, .45-cal. pistol in hand, but by the time he reached the Panther, the crew had run away under the cover of the smoke. German troops from nearby buildings fired at Bizien, and he was mortally wounded. The other tanks of the *détachement* entered the Tuileries garden, fighting against a pair of Panthers. By the end of the afternoon, four of the five Shermans that had led the advance down the Rue de Rivoli had been knocked out of action and all of the Panthers had been destroyed.

LEFT
Some of the most intense fighting of the day took place around the Palais du Luxembourg, seat of the French Senate, and the surroundinging Luxembourg gardens. This shows the courtyard of the palace after the surrender of the German garrison late in the day with a lone Renault FT light tank in the center. (NARA)

BELOW LEFT
German prisoners are escorted away by an FFI group. The Wehrmacht troops preferred to surrender to regular French Army units than the FFI because of their better discipline. (NARA)

recognized that such action would ensure bitter relations between France and Germany once the war had ended. Choltitz was a good enough soldier to understand that the war would not last much longer and that Germany would be subject to the wrath of the Allies. The destruction of Paris was not in Germany's interest, regardless of Hitler's malevolence.

The fighting continued in many parts of Paris through Friday afternoon. The city streets were a bewildering confusion of celebrations and sporadic gunfire. The last major stronghold to surrender was the Palais du Luxembourg, held by diehards with several tanks. They were ordered by

V Corps storms Paris: August 24, 1944

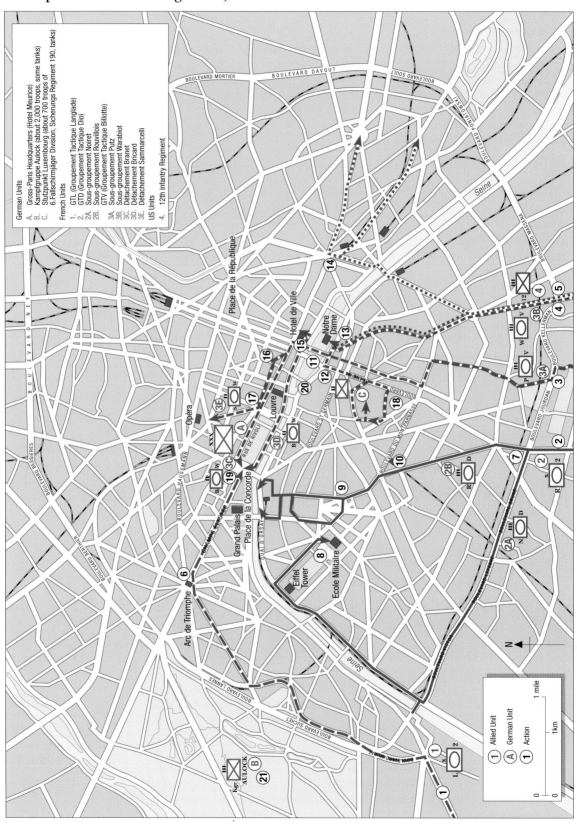

German Units

- A. Gross-Paris Headquarters (Hotel Meurice)
- B. Kampfgruppe Aulock (about 2,000 troops, some tanks)
- C. Stutzpunkt Luxembourg (about 700 troops of
    6.Fallschirmjäger Division, Sicherungs Regiment 190, tanks)

French Units

- 1. GTL (Groupement Tactique Langlade)
- 2. GTD (Groupement Tactique Dio)
- 2A. Sous-groupement Noiret
- 2B. Sous-groupement Rouvillois
- 2B. GTV (Groupement Tactique Billotte)
- 3A. Sous-groupement Putz
- 3B. Sous-groupement Warabiot
- 3C. Détachement Branet
- 3D. Détachement Bricard
- 3E. Détachement Sammarcelli

US Units

- 4. 12th Infantry Regiment

Choltitz' officers to surrender, and, after firing off their ammunition, they capitulated at 1935hrs. In total about 20,000 German troops surrendered on Friday and Saturday, and German casualties during the week of the uprising were estimated at 3,200 soldiers. The 2e DB suffered 42 killed and 77 wounded on Friday, and civilian casualties were later put at 127 dead and 714 wounded. Total 2e DB casualties in the liberation of Paris were later put at 28 officers and about 600 enlisted men killed or wounded; tank losses included 11 destroyed and 11 damaged. De Gaulle appointed Gén. Koenig as the military governor of Paris until civilian order was restored.

CONSECRATION

De Gaulle arrived in the city late on Friday and set up office in the Invalides. He remained anxious about a possible coup by communist elements within the FFI, and snubbed a request to visit the CNR leadership first in the Hôtel de Ville, instead appearing at the police prefecture where the uprising had begun. His plan was to make a formal entry to the city on Saturday, August 25, with a visit to the Tomb of the Unknown Soldier at the Arc de Triomphe, then a procession down the Champs Élysées to Notre Dame cathedral for a celebratory mass. The city was still in a state of turmoil with a significant number of German troops on the loose and some threat from German forces outside the city. As a result, de Gaulle assigned Leclerc's 2e DB the honor of providing the guard for the celebrations. Major-General Leonard Gerow was largely unaware of these arrangements and had issued orders of the day for the 2e DB to take part in operations pushing the Allied lines out to the

V Corps storms Paris: August 24, 1944

1 Groupement Tactique L departs Porte de Sévres area around 0700hrs leaving behind a detachment to clear out the Renault factory in the area.

2 Groupement Tactique D begins its advance around 0700hrs towards Porte d'Orleans

3 Groupement Tactique V begins moving around 0730hrs Warabiot's *sous-groupement* from Porte de Gentilly

4 Putz's *sous-groupement* from GTV begins moving out from Porte d'Italie around 0700hrs.

5 12th Infantry Regiment begins movement around dawn toward Porte d'Italie, led by elements of the 102nd Cavalry Group

6 Aside from an encounter with an anti-tank gun in a bunker at the corner of Rue de Longchamp, GTL arrives largely unopposed at the Arc de Triomphe in late morning; a detachment is sent to capture the nearby German headquarters in the Hotel Majestic.

7 After reaching Porte d'Orleans, GTD splits in two with Noiret's *sous-groupement* moving down the southern side of the city, then passing up the east side of the Seine.

8 Noiret's *sous-groupement* traverses the Champ de Mars aside the Eiffel Tower by late morning, and proceeds to attack and capture the École Militaire.

9 Rouvillois' *sous-groupement* captures the Invalides in late morning, and then in the afternoon sends smaller detachments toward the Quai d'Orsay to seize important government buildings.

10 Leclerc had planned to set up headquarters at the Hotel Crillon, but instead sets up his command post in the Gare Montparnasse train station.

11 Sous-groupement Warabiot makes a rapid advance toward the Île de la Cité, and reaches the police prefecture around 0830hrs.

12 Sous-groupement Putz covers the eastern side of the GTV and reaches the Seine river along the Quai de Montebello where it waits for further instructions.

13 A detachment from the 12th Infantry Regiment reaches Notre Dame around 0830hrs.

14 The main body of the 12th Infantry Regiment heads across the Seine for Gare d'Austerlitz where its battalions fan out to establish an eastern perimeter for V Corps with plans to meet up with other units crossing the Seine farther east.

15 When Choltitz refuses the first surrender offer, at 1300hrs the Warabiot *sous-groupement* breaks into three détachements to attack the German headquarters at the Hotel Meurice. Bricard's détachement of two mechanized infantry platoons and a tank platoon moves along the north bank of the Seine and deals with the threat of German tanks in the Tuilerries gardens.

16 Branet's *détachement* consisting of two tank and two mechanized infantry platoons makes the main thrust down Rue de Rivoli, taking control of Hotel Meurice around 1400hrs. Choltitz agrees to surrender.

17 The Sammarcelli *détachement* of two mechanized infantry platoons and one tank platoon supports the Branet *détachement* by advancing in parallel along Rue St. Honoré, and storming Hotel Meurice from the other side. Once this was accomplished, the *détachement* heads out to take control of the German Kommendatura on Place de l'Opéra.

18 Leclerc realizes that the large concentration of German troops in and around the Luxembourg gardens and the senate pose the last remaining threat. Putz's *sous-groupement* sets out to attack the Senate around 1330–1400hrs, arriving first at the École des Mines on the south east side of the gardens around 1500hrs. The German troops are cleared out of the gardens and the Senate by 1800hrs.

19 After clearing out the tanks in the Tuileries gardens, GTL and GTV meet up on the Place de la Concorde around 1500–1600hrs.

20 Choltitz is taken to the police prefecture to formally sign the surrender. German officers are dispatched to remaining German outposts in Paris to instruct them to surrender.

21 Aulock's Kampfgruppe in the Bois de Boulogne is the last remaining hold out of the Paris garrison, and is not included in the surrender document.

northern suburbs of the city. Relations between Gerow and Leclerc had started off on the wrong foot with the Guillebon affair, and turned hostile because of a string of misunderstandings over the operations in Paris. Gerow sent instructions that the 2e DB was not to take part in the parade and reminded Leclerc that he was under V Corps' command and not to take instructions from other sources, meaning de Gaulle. Leclerc was caught in an unpleasant predicament and tried to avoid a confrontation by disappearing from his headquarters to avoid receiving the instructions. A US colonel finally tracked down Leclerc and de Gaulle at a restaurant near the Invalides and warned that if the division participated in the parade, it would be a "formal breach of military discipline" to which de Gaulle coldly replied that "I loaned you Leclerc; I can perfectly well borrow him back for a few minutes."

In spite of the squabbling by senior commanders, the mood on the street was ecstatic. The revered US war correspondent Ernie Pyle remarked that it was as impossible to describe the mood in Paris "as to describe a desert sunrise in black and white."

The procession of de Gaulle and the other officers and resistance leaders began in mid-afternoon at the Arc de Triomphe and made its way down the Champs Élysées with throngs of Parisians lining the street; some estimates

General von Choltitz is interrogated by the US Army shortly after the surrender on August 25. (NARA)

put the crowd at two million out of a city population of about four million. The parade was not without its dangers, and when de Gaulle reached the Place de la Concorde, a shot rang out. It would not be the last shot of the day, though it remains unclear if this was a German sniper or an overexcited FFI member shooting at imaginary enemies.

The firing started again when de Gaulle reached Notre Dame, and the 2e DB troops began firing at the steeples. De Gaulle ignored the stray bullets and the officers tried to restore order. On entering the cathedral, firing continued even inside. As the congregation took cover from the rifle fire, the imperious general strode down the aisle, seemingly oblivious to the danger around himself. De Gaulle's undoubted displays of courage that day cemented his legend in French history and well served his plans to create a popularly accepted government to replace the despised Pétain regime.

It remains a mystery who was involved in the numerous outbreaks of sniping on the Saturday. Some attributed it to the pro-Vichy Milice, to the Germans, to inexperienced FFI members and to the communists. Regardless of the source, Général Koenig concluded that the worst danger in Paris that weekend was not the Germans but the undisciplined FFI. The FFI had swelled from a few thousand disciplined and highly motivated insurgents at the start of the uprising, to over 20,000 with no centralized control. Armed bands were roaming the city, dispensing summary justice against captured Germans, as well as French men and women accused of collaboration. There was some concern that fighting could break out between armed militias, and so both de Gaulle and Koenig concluded that the best solution would be to put the FFI in uniform and subject them to military discipline. The PCF attempted to set up a Milice Populaire under the control of the COMAC, but de Gaulle

Under the terms of the surrender, German officers were sent around the city to order the holdouts to surrender. This jeep was sent to the Senate in the Palais du Luxembourg to end the fighting there in the late afternoon. (MHI)

De Gaulle leads the procession down the Champs Élysées during the victory parade on August 25, behind him and in the center, Gén. Jacques Leclerc, and to his side the newly appointed military governor of Paris, Gén. Pierre Koenig. (NARA)

bluntly told them that there was no need for such a force. De Gaulle's concern about the chaos in Paris was serious enough that he asked Eisenhower to leave the 2e DB in the city for the time being and add two more divisions for good measure. Neither Bradley nor Eisenhower wanted one of their armored divisions tied up with police tasks, but, under the circumstances, there was little option. The 28th Infantry Division was assigned to take over the 2e DB's front on the northwest side of Paris. Eisenhower also agreed to have the division parade down the Champs Élysées on its way to the front, in part as a victory celebration, but also as a show of force to emphasize that the US Army stood behind de Gaulle and the new provisional government. This impromptu gesture became one of the most vivid symbols of the US Army's campaign in the liberation of Europe with positive repercussions far beyond Eisenhower's expectations.

THE GERMAN REACTION

On Friday as the 2e DB was entering Paris, Hitler demanded of Jodl, chief of the general staff: "Brennt Paris?"—"Is Paris burning?" Jodl didn't know and the inquiry went down the chain of command. On learning of the capitulation of Paris the next day, Hitler ordered the city retaken. In the meantime, he

LEFT
An M9 half-track of the 3/RMT
heads down the Champs
Élysées during the victory
parade on the afternoon
of August 25. (NARA)

BELOW LEFT
The crowds dash for cover
when sporadic firing breaks
out on the Place de la
Concorde on August 25 as de
Gaulle's procession advanced
from the Champs Élysées
toward Notre Dame cathedral.
(NARA)

ordered that all available V-weapons be launched against the city, and that the Luftwaffe obliterate the city by bombing attack. The Luftwaffe staged a bombing raid on Saturday night, August 26, hitting the eastern side of the city, killing 213 people and injuring a further 914. At the time, the V-1 sites was in the process of evacuating the bases in the Pas de Calais so none were fired against Paris. The V-2 batteries were only beginning to deploy in the Netherlands, so their participation in the bombardment was perfunctory. Only four missiles were launched starting on 6 September 1944 of which only one hit the suburbs southeast of Paris on September 8, killing six people and injuring a further 36.

The victory parade ended on the Île de la Cité near where the Paris uprising began, at Notre Dame cathedral. Random sniping even within the church was a reminder that Paris, though liberated, was still not at peace. (NARA)

Combat action on the ground against Paris was made difficult by the rout of German forces throughout northern France. AOK 1 was desperately trying to hold back the US Army's Seine River bridgeheads on either side of Paris. The only immediate reserve in the area was the Panzer Lehr Division, which was being rebuilt after its decimation in Normandy, and newly arriving elements of the 47.Infanterie Division. The assignment from Berlin was for the Panzer Lehr Division to send tanks into the center of the city, while the 47.Infanterie Division was assigned to create a barrier from Montmorency toward Champigny. The orders were wildly unrealistic and all that the Panzer Lehr Division could muster was a small *Kampfgruppe* under Hauptmann Hennecke from I Bataillon, Panzergrenadier Regiment 901, with about 800 troops, reinforced with a company of Panther tanks from Panzer Regiment 6 and some heavy infantry guns. The *Kampfgruppe* set out for Paris on the late evening of Friday, August 24, heading for Le Bourget. After moving through the airport, the *Kampfgruppe* proceeded into the city at a snail's pace because of the barricades and frequent encounters with snipers. Some elements of the group claim to have reached as far as the Gare du Nord railway station, but under the circumstances the unit withdrew from the city to the northeast rather than face the wrath of inflamed Parisians. The airport area was the scene of considerable fighting on August 27–28, involving elements of the 4th Infantry Division, 2e DB and local FFI units. AOK 1 later attempted to create a cordon around the city directed by LVII Panzer Korps controlling elements of the 348.Infanterie Division and other available formations. In reality, the tempo of the operations was dependent entirely on the US Army's actions.

After the 28th Infantry Division conducted its parade through Paris on August 29 it moved into the line north of the city alongside the 5th Armored Division to the west and 4th Infantry Division to the east. German resistance for the most part was perfunctory as by this stage the Wehrmacht was in an almost complete rout along this sector of the front, a period Wehrmacht commanders later dubbed "the void." With Paris overcoming its victory hangover, V Corps began to advance and, by early September, had reached the Belgian border, heading for the Siegfried Line.

Relations between Leclerc and Gerow had become so bad during the Paris operation that de Gaulle approached Eisenhower and Bradley about shifting the division back to Patton's Third Army, and preferably Haislip's XV Corps. Both Patton and Haislip had studied at French war colleges in the 1920s, were fluent in French, and were more understanding of French circumstances than Gerow. Leclerc was anxious to get his unit out of Paris as the occupation duties tended to lead to widespread desertion and other problems. On September 3, the 2e DB was transferred to Patton's Third Army and later in the month would engage in one of its most successful battles, against Panzer Brigade 112 at Dompaire in Lorraine. Its role in the liberation of Strasburg later in the year cemented its place in French legend.

In a rage over Choltitz's failure to destroy Paris, Hitler ordered the Luftwaffe to obliterate the city. Although one major raid was conducted, the German bomber force was in no shape to conduct a sustained campaign. This He-177 heavy bomber was captured at the airbase near Châteaudun on the approaches to Paris in August 1944. (NARA)

AFTERMATH

Hitler's assessment of the importance of Paris was fundamentally mistaken; France did not fall because of the loss of Paris, Paris was lost because of the fall of France. The last two weeks of August 1944 saw the total collapse of the Wehrmacht in France. While some areas remained in German control—the Saar, Lorraine, Alsace—most of France was liberated. The Wehrmacht lost some 300,000 troops killed and captured plus a further 200,000 stranded in the *Festung* ports by Hitler's stand-fast orders. Nor was the catastrophe yet over. The rapid and deep penetration of Allied armies led to further encirclements in Belgium in early September 1944.

Paris was spared the fate of Warsaw by the magnanimity of Eisenhower and the US Army and the stubborn promotion of French interests by de Gaulle and the other Free French leaders. Eisenhower viewed de Gaulle as troublesome and vainglorious, but sincere and profoundly patriotic. Eisenhower and Bradley could have dawdled and asked Washington's permission to liberate Paris; instead they made a snap decision to intervene to prevent needless destruction. From first-hand experience, Eisenhower had

French collaborators were the target of FFI patrols and angry mobs seeking retribution. To prevent the spread of mob violence, de Gaulle insisted that the FFI come under strict military command. (NARA)

LEFT
The jubilant reaction of
Parisians to the liberation
remains one of the most vivid
memories of US soldiers in
World War II, an affirmation
of the "good war." (NARA)

BELOW
While Eisenhower was
unwilling to deploy any US
troops to police Paris, he did
authorize the parade of the
28th Infantry Division on
August 29 during its move
to the northern suburbs of
Paris as a way of reaffirming
US support for de Gaulle's
fledgling government. (NARA)

A column of the 28th Infantry Division marches down the Champs Élysées with the Arc de Triomphe visible in the background during the August 29 parade. (NARA)

a better sense of the will of the French people than bureaucrats back in Washington, and so helped foster the rebirth of a new democratic French state. De Gaulle's incessant promotion of the French cause since 1940 and the heroism of the French resistance in 1944 were essential ingredients in shaping Eisenhower's decisions. For the US Army, the liberation of Paris was a magnificent conclusion to the bruising summer campaign in Normandy. The ecstatic French crowds in Paris strongly reinforced the popular perception that this was a "good war" worth the bloody sacrifice of Omaha Beach and the grim hedgerow battles in Normandy.

For France, the liberation of Paris was a glorious redemption after the humiliating defeat of 1940 and the disgraceful years of occupation and collaboration. The legends of resistance helped cloud the memories of years of sordid accommodation with the Wehrmacht. Born in the exciting days of uprising and liberation, the new Fourth Republic descended to the petty politics of the prewar Third Republic, ending in ignominy with the Indo-Chinese and Algerian crises in the 1950s. In a reprise in his role as national savior, de Gaulle returned in 1958, creating today's Fifth Republic.

THE BATTLEFIELD TODAY

The liberation of Paris in 1944 has become one of the core events in modern French history, and it takes very little effort to find reminders all over Paris. Most of the prominent buildings associated with the 1944 rising in Paris still exist; the police prefecture still has bullet holes visible. The Grand Palais was rebuilt after the 1944 fire and next to it is the monument of de Gaulle striding down the Champs Élysées. There are numerous museums and monuments situated around Paris commemorating the 1944 uprising. Hardly a town in the region lacks a street commemorating "Août 1944." Almost as numerous are streets dedicated in memory of the legendary "2e DB." Although not the most conspicuous, some of the most touching memorials in Paris are the

In memory of his legendary walk down the Champs Élysées, Paris erected a statue of de Gaulle on a plinth adjacent to the Grand Palais at Place Clemenceau. (Author's collection)

The Paris uprising gained momentum with the seizure of the police prefecture located on the Île de la Cité in the heart of city. The prefecture is much the same today as in 1944, and is located near the legendary Notre Dame cathedral seen here in the background to the right. (Author's collection)

plaques scattered through the city to the fallen dead of the FFI, executed by the Germans or killed in the 1944 uprising. The "Mémorial du Maréchal Leclerc de Hauteclocque et de la Libération de Paris" was unveiled in 1994 on the 50th anniversary near the Montparnasse railroad station where Leclerc had his headquarters on August 24; there is an associated library located appropriately enough at 23 Allée de la 2e DB near the Jardin Atlantique. The Musée de l'Armée in the Invalides added a display dedicated to de Gaulle and the FFI in 2000. The Musée de la Résistance Nationale dedicated to the work of the CPL and COMAC was established in 1985 in Champigny-sur-Marne, with a research library added in 1994.

FURTHER READING

The liberation of Paris is covered in many accounts of the summer of 1944 fighting, but there have been surprisingly few specialized studies. The standard French account is the Dansette study that has been reprinted over the years in many editions. The most popular account is Collins and Lapierre's bestseller, *Is Paris Burning?*; it remains a good read but marred by over-dramatization and fuzzy if not inaccurate details of the military aspects of the event. The associated movie based on the book is not bad compared with other Hollywood blockbusters of the time. It is reasonably faithful to the book, though the casting is at times rather strange, such as Kirk Douglas as Patton. From the US perspective, there is a substantial amount of material on the operation scattered through the memoirs, unit histories and campaign accounts. The V Corps official history contains most of the relevant orders and key documents. The day-by-day 12th Army Group situation maps are available at the Library of Congress. A remarkable collection of transcribed reports of the 7th Armored Division are located on Wesley Johnston's Internet site (http://home.comcast.net/~johnstonww/index.htm)

Some of the most detailed accounts of the fighting for the Seine bridgeheads around Paris are provided in French regional histories such as the Renoult and Lodieu books on the Mantes bridgehead, and the Santin book on the fighting for Chartres. There is an enormous amount of material on the Paris events in French, and several books on the 2e DB. Documentation from the German side is less extensive than the Allied side as the records of AOK 1 and the 325.Sicherungs Division appear to have been lost. Choltitz' autobiography appeared in 1964 in both German and French. One of his regimental commanders, Hans Jay, also wrote a recollection of the Paris events though it appears to be aimed more as a retort to the Collins and Lapierre book and it is not particularly well detailed on the military aspects of the campaign. Fortunately, there is some very good coverage of the campaign in the US Army's Foreign Military Studies written after the war by German officers; I used the collection at the US Army Military History Institute at Carlisle Barracks in Pennsylvania.

US ARMY FOREIGN MILITARY STUDIES

Boineberg-Longsfeld, Hans Freiherr von, *Northern France: 325th Security Division* (A-967)

Boineberg-Longsfeld, Hans Freiherr von, *Organization of the Defense of Paris* (B-015)

Emmerich, Albert, *Northern France—First Army August–September 1944* (B-728)

Hesse, Kurt, *Defense of Paris—Summer 1944* (B-611)

Krause, Ernst von, *Military Governor—France* (B-612)

Schramm, Percy, *OKW War Diary 11 April–16 December 1944: The West* (B-034)

Souchay, Curt, *Seventh and First Army Rear Areas, August–September 1944* (A-900)

Ziegelmann, Fritz, *Resistance Movement in the West* (B-022)

US ARMY STUDIES

V Corps Operations in the ETO, 6 Jan 1942–9 May 1945 (1946)

XII Corps: Spearhead of Patton's Third Army, (1947)

XIX Tactical Air Command's First Month of Operations in Support of Third US Army in France (1944)

Lewis, S. J., *Jedburgh Team Operations in Support of the 12th Army Group, August 1944,* (Combat Studies Institute: 1991)

The Cross of Lorraine: A Combat History of the 79th Infantry Division, June 1942–December 1945, (n.d.)

The Saga of XX "Ghost Corps" Thru Hell and Highwater (n.d.)

World War II: A Chronology, August 1944 (War Department Historical Division, 1946)

BOOKS

Bradley, Omar, *A Soldier's Story* (Henry Holt, 1951)

Blumenson, Martin, *Breakout and Pursuit* (CMH, 1961)

Choltitz, Dietrich von, *Un soldat parmi des soldats* (Aubanel, 1964)

Clayton, Anthony, *Three Marshals of France: Leadership After Trauma* (Brassey's, 1992)

Collins, Larry, and Lapierre, D., *Is Paris Burning?* (Simon & Schuster, 1965)

Dansette, Adrien, *Histoire de la Libération de Paris* (Fayard, 1946)

Eymard, Alain, *2e DB* (Heimdal, 1990)

Foot, M. R. D., *SOE in France* (HMSO, 1966)

Hogan, David, *A Command Post at War: First Army HQ in Europe 1943–45* (CMH, 2000)

Jay, Hans, *Erinnerungen an den II. Weltkrieg* (self-published, 1970)

Knight, Frida, *The French Resistance* (Lawrence & Wishart, 1975)

Lacouture, Jean, *De Gaulle: The Rebel 1890–1944* (Wm. Collins, 1990)

Lodieu, Didier, *Combats sur la Seine* (Ysec, 2006)

Marcot, François, et al. *Dictionnaire historique de la Résistance* (Laffont, 2006)

Perrigault, Jean-Claude, *La Panzer-Lehr Division* (Heimdal, 1995)

Pittino, Henri, *Combats de la 2e DB en Normandie* (Muller, 2002)

Pryce-Jones, David, *Paris in the Third Reich* (Holt, Rinehart & Winston, 1981)

Renoult, Bruno, *1944 Guerre en Île de France, Vol. 1: Les preparatifs* (Histoire vivant, 2006)

Renoult, Bruno, Havelvange, G., *La bataille du Vexin* (Trame, 2004)

Renoult, Bruno, Havelvange, G., *La tête de pont de Mantes* (Trame, 2000)

Rocheteau, Jean, *Paris Libéré 19–27 août 1944* (Batailles Hors-série numero 2, 2004)

Santin, Eric, *1944 Eure-et-Loir: Derniers Combats* (self-published, 2001)

The 4th Infantry "Ivy" Division: Steadfast & Loyal (Turner, 1987)

The Lucky Seventh: The 7th Armored Division (Taylor, 1982)

Thornton, Willis, *The Liberation of Paris* (Harcourt, Brace, 1962)

INDEX